THE ENDLESS JOURNEY

A UNIQUE PERSPECTIVE ON MANKIND'S
ORIGIN, PURPOSE AND ULTIMATE DESTINY

DAVID V. GAGGIN

ISBN 10: 1484982215
ISBN 13: 978-1484982211
Library of Congress Control Number: 2013909633
CreateSpace Independent Publishing Platform
North Charleston, SC

TABLE OF CONTENTS

PREFACE

Our history is a myth and our myths are history.

– Unknown

Mankind's greatest longing is to know the meaning of life. We all have a need to know:

Who are we?
Are we important?
Why are we here?
Is there life after death?
Is there a God?
If so, does he care about us?
Most importantly, how should we live our lives?

If we had answers to these questions, we would have a much greater understanding of ourselves and the world we live in and be able to make better decisions in life. We each have a worldview, a way in which we see the world and how we fit into it from a unique and personal perspective; a view we rarely share with others. Yet, few of us appreciate that our worldviews go a long way in defining who we are and how we deal with the many issues that we face. Our worldviews make life meaningful, futile, or very often leaves us in a confusing in-between state. Our views are initially handed down to us from our parents or guardians; influenced by one or more religious doctrines; maybe altered by science; and further altered by personal pursuits into philosophy, metaphysics, or so forth. Each of us has thought about life and death to some extent, and some of us have thought about them a great deal; however, most people consider the issue too difficult to understand, so they either follow a preexisting religious or scientific doctrine or simply ignore it completely. Most people, if asked about their worldview, would either quote a religious doctrine or offer a vague statement about not being sure. Very few of us have spent time trying to understand or develop our worldviews to the point that we can articulate what we truly believe, let alone why we believe it. The older we get, the harder it is to ignore the reality of death; we simply want to know what, if anything, is next.

Our worldviews shape our lives by controlling our actions in everything we do. They determine our views on social issues like abortion and gay rights; religious issues like following Christianity, Buddhism, Hinduism, etc.; how we feel about people that do not look like us; and even what our goals are and how we treat one another. Our worldviews dictate how we live, how we act, and what we think. We cannot live a life without making certain basic assumptions about who we are and what is important to us. Our worldviews greatly influence who and what we become.

Although science answers many of our day-to-day issues and surely provides many material benefits, it only focuses on the material world. As such, it tells us life is simply a sophisticated group of chemical reactions, and when we die, it is over; our existence comes to an end. Science's worldview is that the universe miraculously came into being without transcendent help and will eventually evaporate into meaningless chaos. The implications of such a view could easily support a selfish existence as being our best choice; live life large and get what we can.

If we turn to theology for a worldview, we get a different story. We are told that we are spiritual beings that need salvation, and each religion has a different view of what being saved means. Christianity claims man is sinful, and a belief in Jesus Christ will solve the problem. Judaism and Islam believe that salvation comes from living a life consistent with God's wishes and we will be judged how well we did at death. Hinduism and Buddhism believe salvation results from living a selfless life as we are being punished for sins of previous lives. Most religions take a transcendent perspective of the material world and believe that there is life after death, and God is the divine judge of our behavior; if he disapproves, punishment awaits at death's door. None of these views are very satisfying, and in my opinion they all rely on illogical arguments that distort their perspectives. Unfortunately the extensions of some of these worldviews can be extremely self-destructive, and even the most comforting of views leave most of us wondering how to live our lives.

It is highly unlikely that any of these worldviews are accurate, although they each surely incorporate some reality. Our greatest thinkers have been addressing these issues since the beginning of recorded history. Although it is impossible to scientifically prove the answers to the questions posed above, we do not need to rely on blind faith either. Despite what we have been told, there is a great deal of information available that can shed light on these questions, and it is readily accessible to anyone willing to search for it. This information comes from scientific, theological, philosophical, and historical texts, but it is not well-known because it goes against most religious and scientific doctrines.

It is my opinion that there is enough evidence available to convince even the most skeptical mind that many of the answers to the questions regarding life's purpose can be found during our lifetimes. The more skeptical the seeker, the more tedious and complete the search must be, but in the end it is only the seeker that can determine what to believe. I cannot stress enough that *nothing comes without effort*, and jumping to a conclusion is a difficult way to find truth. Although truth is hidden from us in this life, it is not kept from us. The purpose of seeking is to understand what is important, who we are, and how we fit into the grander scheme of life. It is by definition a personal journey, and to take this journey requires several things.

The first, which may be the hardest for some of us, is to start with an open mind and put aside our prejudices. We have all been bombarded with false premises for so long that we consider them factual, often for lack of better ideas. These concepts have become basic assumptions and may be our biggest stumbling blocks. Letting them go is often a bit scary because we don't know what we will find. It is like throwing away a crutch before we know we can walk. We believe many things simply because we want to, and they make us feel good—or at least we think they do—but if they are not true, what value do they have? We often put our opinions above those of others and use our prejudices as an excuse to think less of them. We associate with people with similar beliefs because they reinforce the dogmas to which we cling. We owe it to ourselves to seek truth, and we can only do this by continually challenging our beliefs.

Secondly, we need the self-confidence to believe that we can make our own decisions and not depend on others to tell us what is true. We start out in life with our parents telling us what to believe; then it is our teachers, our clergy, and our doctors. We get a job, and our bosses and peers tell us what to do, and in some cases even what to think. We watch television and read newspapers and books, and the talking heads and journalists all tell us what to believe. We are so inundated with opinion sold as truth that we become accustomed to depending on others to tell us what to believe. Inherently we know that much of it is nonsense, but it is hard going against the crowd. We rationalize that: "This must be true because so many smart people believe it, although it doesn't really make sense to me"; but those smart people are thinking the same thing. If we cannot rationally explain our beliefs to ourselves, then we need to admit that our beliefs are more opinion than truth. If we are going to search for truth, we need to be prepared to decide for ourselves what truth really is. We will know truth when we see it, as it will resonate with our subconscious minds; it will feel right. We have been given the gifts of reason and discrimination, and we are obliged to use these gifts. Taking responsibility for what we believe is a major step toward freedom.

Thirdly, we need to understand what constitutes proof. The scientific community likes to tell people who subscribe to differing ideas that they have no proof; however, the reality is that science has never proved anything yet. They come up with hypotheses on which they perform limited tests. They then create general principles and call this proof until someone finds a circumstance in which the prediction does not work, which is pretty common. Physics and chemistry, which are considered the hard sciences, are forever changing their truths, and there is no reason to think they have too much of it right as of yet. The softer sciences like astronomy and biology do not even do as well, and the really soft sciences like archeology, psychology, and climatology are simply flailing at the truth. Scientific proofs have a very short half-life. Religion, on the other hand, makes only the feeblest attempt to prove anything and when challenged quickly turns to faith for its rationale. Although religion builds up faith as a wonderful thing, blind faith, which is the basis of so many religions, is hardly a solid foundation for our worldview. Proof is an opinion that we have convinced ourselves is correct, and as such, it is all in the eye of the beholder. Truth is what is real and has little to do with what we think has been proved. The best we can do is to use reason and discrimination, coupled with open minds, and then decide on the most plausible explanation. The key, of course, is always being on the lookout for contradictory ideas. Truth is when science, religion, and philosophy come together. No matter how we parse it, the truth will always be consistent from every perspective.

Finally, we need the desire to know truth and the will to search for it. Living in the age of information has its advantages and disadvantages. The good news is that truth is readily available to us, but the bad news is that it is buried in a background of noise. Searching through the massive amount of data and following an untold number of dead-end streets is a daunting task that only a relative few have chosen to pursue; however, no one can search for us. Each of us needs to find our own truth. I cannot guarantee that you will find the same answers that I did or even that indeed my view of truth is correct. What I can guarantee is that anyone who truly and rigorously pursues truth will develop a whole new perspective on the world and on himself or herself. The personal rewards attained from this newfound perspective will be immense, but remember, truth is only acquired through effort.

The ideas in this book did not originate with me. I have had no revealed knowledge or unusual experiences on which I have based these accounts. All of the information that I have studied and included in this book is readily available to anyone who chooses to pursue it. I have searched through an enormous amount of data and numerous different accounts and perspectives. Of particular help were accounts from people that have had specific insights into what we would all refer to as the spiritual world. These inputs come from all walks of life, down through the ages, and across many different disciplines. By looking at these inputs, I was able to put together a story describing reality that is very different from mainstream thought. What I found so amazing is how consistent the various supporting stories are despite the disparate inputs and time frames.

In our search for truth, it is critical to understand that each of us has our own prejudices and biases, and these must be purged or weighed accordingly. I cannot guarantee that my summation is completely factual to the minutest degree, especially as I have my own biases, but I believe that my view articulates a rational and realistic picture of who we are and why we are here and provides a guide to assist all of us in how to live our lives. This book is not meant to provide the reader with the answers to life, as each of us must search out those answer for ourselves. My hope is that for those of you that are either ready to begin your search or have already begun, you may gain an insight and a direction as to where to search next and how you might move forward on your own journey.

I have written this book in such a manner that you do not have to wade through all my tedious research and rationale on every topic to discover my conclusions. Much of my early searching and investigating was filled with confusion and doubt, and I realized that to attempt to drag you through the process would be hopelessly complicated, and in the end it would not add to the content of the book. I have chosen to provide only selected rationale where I believe the concepts are especially important and go against many people's belief systems. In some instances, I simply point the reader to references where further understanding can be found. Numerous books have been written on every topic I discuss, and to assist those who want to investigate additional areas of interest, I have provided a bibliography and an additional suggested reading list.

I have included a number of items that I consider asides, as they are not specifically required to achieve understanding of the theme and focus of the book; however, they are topics that I wondered about and pursued for years before finally understanding their meaning. These aside items include astrology, enlightenment, akashic records, the Holy Grail, the kabbalah, and a number of other topics. I have briefly discussed these topics in the hope that by including them I can assist others who have also been pondering them. Although I believe these items add depth to my perspective, they are not critical to the book. Readers that want to conduct further research on these topics will find reference material in the suggested reading list.

My objectives in writing this book are to: (1) offer new ideas or perspectives of which you may not have thought; (2) entice you to believe that answers can be found on issues commonly believed unanswerable in this lifetime; (3) help you understand your own personal journey; (4) show that you and only you have the power to improve your life; and most of all, (5) encourage you to see yourself as a special being with an incredibly bright future who brings a unique and valuable perspective to the universe.

Readers who are ready for knowledge need no encouragement. Only those who seek truth will find it and learn about themselves in the process, and only those that know themselves will align themselves with the cosmos and grow comfortably within it. Enjoy life and treat yourself well. You have earned it!

INTRODUCTION

Wisdom we gained from the star-born races, wisdom and knowledge far beyond man. Down to us had descended the masters of wisdom as far beyond us as I am from thee. List ye now while I give ye wisdom. Use it and free thou shalt be.

– The Emerald Tablets[1]

As a teenager I was extremely interested in understanding the world around me, and science was always a fascination; however, its view that we were no more than a compilation of molecules and that chemical processes were what made us self-aware seemed extremely shortsighted to me. Although I was not sure if life went on after death, science's total disregard for the spirit was unsettling.

I was introduced to religion through Episcopalian Christianity, and although the spirit was discussed in these teachings, the pomp and ceremony and doctrine were front and center. I did not see Christianity as a spiritual experience, but more of a ritualistic encounter. When I talked to ministers and other churchgoers and tried to find out why they believed

---

1   See the glossary for information on the Emerald Tablets.

the Christian doctrine was truth, no one could provide me with answers that could satisfy my doubts. No one wanted to talk about the intellectual aspects of Christianity; they would only recite scripture or give me books to read. I dutifully read the books, hoping to find an insight that I had overlooked, but I found no revelations. I found stories of how people's faith helped them through difficult times, confirmation of people's belief and assurance of its truth, but never any rational argument of why it was true; all I found were platitudes. It seemed that people believed because they either were afraid not to believe or did not know what else to believe. The people I talked to felt a need to believe in something greater than themselves, and since they were raised to associate Christianity with God, they were Christians. It was clear to me as a teenager that no one could explain Christianity to my satisfaction.

As a young adult I was consumed by education, a career, and raising a family, but I still continued my search at every opportunity. I looked at the other major religions and found new concepts like reincarnation and karma but had no real feel for whether these were true or just wishful thinking. The Eastern religions seemed to be more philosophical than the Abrahamic religions, but they were difficult to understand as well. It seemed that every religion had so many splinter sects following divergent doctrines that I could believe anything I wanted and still call myself a "whatever." As a young man, I found that religion simply did not work for me.

I was an electrical engineer by training and profession, so science was a natural place for me to search for answers. I liked all science; astronomy, physics, chemistry, anthropology, archeology, and biology were all of great interest to me. It seemed that science wanted logical facts, and that was what I was looking for. Einstein's relativity theory and Bohr's quantum mechanics were fascinating and made me realize that the world was not as it appeared to be. The physical laws of the macroworld that we lived in were no longer valid when parameters like speed and size were considered. The world around us only appeared as it did because we viewed it through our five senses, which created our reality. This was quite a bombshell for me; the world we knew only existed because of a unique set of circumstances that allowed us to perceive it that way.

I wondered how the very special circumstances needed to create this universe just happened to occur; it seemed unlikely that it was happenstance like science proclaimed. I soon began wondering exactly how unbiased science really was. I began questioning what science called truth. For example, the big bang was proposed as the basis for our existence, yet no one had any reasonable theory of what caused the big bang or what came before it, let alone why it occurred. I wondered how we could have a theory of creation when we had no concept of the cause. I soon realized that science was focused only on interpreting the phenomena within the cosmos. If there was a spiritual world outside of the cosmos, science was not looking for it, and indeed it was denying its very existence. I knew that if the spiritual world existed, I would need to look beyond mainstream science to find it.

By this time I was totally confused; neither religion nor science was able to provide any rational answers as to where we came from, our purpose in life, or how to live our lives. Then my daughter, Julia, gave me a book by Dr. Brian Weiss titled *Many Lives, Many Masters*. It introduced me to the subject of hypnotic regression. Weiss was a psychiatrist that told of numerous examples of patients that would remember past lives when they were under hypnosis. Although the accounts were fascinating, I was not sure of their credibility. I looked for other books on the same subject and soon realized there were many similar books; this phenomenon was a common occurrence in this type of treatment. I read numerous associated accounts, and they all told the same story. The accounts reported incredible things like people under hypnosis who were fluent in past-life languages that were unknown to them in their present lives. I wondered if these authors were telling the truth, as they all were financially benefitting from their books, so I wanted to discuss this with a doctor in the field who was doing hypnotic regressions but had not written about it. I found such a doctor, and he confirmed that indeed his results were the same. As fascinating and detailed as these accounts were, I realized that accounts of other lives were seen through the eyes of the individual patients and interpreted by the doctor, so results had to be taken with some caution, as the individual biases affected the details. Slowly I began to believe that there was truly something here that needed to be considered. These books were usually in the New Age section of the libraries and bookstores, so I started perusing related subjects and found near-death experiences, out-of-body experiences, and other topics that all seemed to corroborate the hypnotic regression reports. I was not sure what to make of all this, but I was becoming convinced that life was not a dead end as science was insisting.

As a parallel and seemingly unrelated interest in my early life, I was always disturbed by the archeological explanations of the huge number of megalithic sites throughout the world. We were told by mainstream science that these structures were quarried and carried into place by people with minimum technical capability; all muscle and no technology. I could never reconcile how these amazing structures could have been created by a nontechnical society. The Great Pyramid of Giza is a good example. It's base covers thirteen acres that are level to within several inches across its entire area; the stones weigh between one and a hundred tons each; they fit so well together that no mortar was used, and yet you cannot put a piece of paper between them; and if the stones were laid end-to-end, they would encircle the earth at the equator. Yet, there is no nearby quarry that produced them, no chisel marks on them, no tools of any sort left behind that were used to build them. We couldn't build the Great Pyramid of Giza today, but somebody built it approximately five thousand years ago, or maybe before then. There are structures like this all over the world: in Africa, the Middle East, Central and South America, Oceana, and Asia. Some of the stones weigh one thousand tons and have smooth, straight cuts in them that nothing we know of today could have made besides giant power tools or lasers. These megastructures are located at elevations up to 7,900 feet in the Peruvian Andes down to below sea level and were so perfectly cut they had no need for reinforcing steel. I was convinced that whoever built them had technology we do not have today, and they had it all over the earth. Even today the cost to create one of these sites would be prohibitive, yet these people, who we are told were barely beyond the savage stage of human development, were able to achieve it, not just in Egypt, but at hundreds of sites around the world. The archeologists' explanations made no sense to me.

While browsing through an archeology section of a bookstore, I ran across a book titled *Maps of the Ancient Sea Kings* that was written by Charles Hapgood, a professor at Keene State College in Keene, New Hampshire. Hapgood describes various European maps used in the 1500s that depicted detailed drawings of the entire world, including the Antarctic land mass under the ice. Maps like the Piri Reis world map of 1513, the Oronteus Finaeus map of 1531, and Hadji Ahmed world map of 1559 showed incredible detail of the entire world, even though none of those areas had been discovered by Europeans at the time. The most interesting aspect was that the parts of the world supposedly unexplored by known cultures were far more accurate, compared to our modern maps, than the areas that were well-known, like the Mediterranean. Hapgood was able to show that the original source maps (those maps that were used to create these maps) were of much higher quality than the map technology available in 1500s and were created by people whose cartography skills (the process of mathematically projecting global characteristics onto flat maps) were much more sophisticated. The technical issue during the 1500s was that there was no available method to precisely determine longitude, so the length of a degree was unknown and remained unknown for another 250 years. The Oronteus Finaeus map was particularly enlightening, as it showed the Ross Sea in Antarctica without ice. In 1949, on one of the Byrd Antarctic expeditions, Dr. Jack Hough took three core samples of the Rose Sea seabed in Antarctica and analyzed them using the ionium method at the Carnegie Institute in Washington, DC. Hough concluded that the Ross Sea was last ice free six thousand years ago and probably for quite some time before that. This implies the source map for the Oronteus Finaeus map was at least six thousand years old, and possibly much older. Hapgood also located a twelfth-century map of China that showed the same deterioration of mapping skills had occurred between that map and its source. Hapgood concluded that: (1) some civilization mapped the entire world thousands of years ago, and (2) their cartography skills were so sophisticated that they were not able to be replicated until the nineteenth century. I found Hapgood's revelations quite astonishing, and they provided strong enough evidence to convince me that the implications of his maps could not be ignored. I did not know who mapped the world over six thousand years ago, but it must have been a very intelligent civilization, and it must have existed on earth before our civilization's recorded history. Between Hapgood and the megalithic structures, I was beginning to believe the many myths of gods walking the earth might be true.

Eventually it came to my attention that archeologists had discovered some thirty to forty thousand clay tablets that were written some three to five thousand years ago in Sumer, Arcadia, and the surrounding areas in Mesopotamia. Samuel Noah Kramer, Clark Research Professor Emeritus of Assyriology at the University of Pennsylvania, published *History Begins at Sumer*, describing some of his findings regarding Sumer's culture circa 3000 BC. The data is taken from the clay tablets and describes life in Sumer. They had educational systems, a government structure consisting of a two-chamber congress with an upper and lower house that limited the power of the king, libraries, hospitals, pharmacies, a legal system, aquariums, trades, commerce, and agriculture. They performed dentistry and surgical operations, had a detailed knowledge of the body, had beer and wine from the earliest times, used perfumes in the houses, and had shade trees for the gardens. They had musical instruments, songs, poetry, lullabies, epic tales, and funeral chants. They wrestled with all the same types of problems that an advanced society does, like morality, labor issues, cosmology, juvenile delinquency, and literary debates. In short, the Sumerian society by 3000 BC had already been fully developed. There is no history of Sumer's development recorded in any of these tablets. They just came out of nowhere and left us thousands of documents telling us about their lives. They speak of their gods as walking among them, making human types of mistakes, but in general supporting and caring for them. Our archaeologists and historians have labeled that part of their written heritage as myths but seem to have accepted the other portions as truth. Jacquetta Hawkes noted in her book *The First Great Civilizations* that the societies of the Nile River, Mesopotamia, and the Indus Valley appear to have come out of nowhere fully formed. These findings seemed incredible to me, as I had never been exposed to any of this in my formal studies.

Then I stumbled across a set of books by Zecharia Sitchin called the Earth Chronicles. Sitchin was an Azerbaijani-born American archaeologist that spent his entire life researching the myths of worldwide civilizations. Much of his research came from the Sumerian clay tablets, which reside in museums around the world; the Old Testament; Egyptian and other hieroglyphic writings; and Central and South American glyphs. He wrote the Earth Chronicles as a series of books in which he wove together an elaborate tale of the history of mankind. The interesting aspect of what Sitchin does is that he takes the ancient myths, tablets, and other ancient writings at face value. Unlike mainstream archeology, which takes everything that does not fit its present theories as fiction, Sitchin simply retold the story that the ancient texts described. The story goes something like this:

Some five hundred thousand years ago, an alien civilization called the Anunnaki landed on earth. Their purpose was to mine gold because they needed it to repair the atmosphere of their home planet. These beings were not immortal but lived for hundreds of thousands of earth years. Mining for gold was very hard work, and the aliens eventually tired of such a difficult life and looked for other beings to do the work for them. The humanoids living on earth at that time were deemed to be unsatisfactory workers, so they decided to create a new race of workers. They used DNA engineering, and after many trials and errors, eventually found a winning combination by mixing their own genetic structure with that of *Homo erectus*, which resulted in the creation of mankind about 250,000 to 300,000 years ago. Mankind, with the assistance of the Anunnaki, eventually spread throughout the planet. The Anunnaki's constant bickering and fighting caused a great deal of trouble on the earth. At the time of Noah, the Anunnaki engineers realized that a huge worldwide catastrophic flood would take place. The Anunnaki king, Enlil, was disappointed with mankind, so he was willing to let the people die. Enki, Enlil's brother, who was a key figure in creating the human race, wanted to save it despite the king's wishes, so he told Noah how to build the ark. After the flood, Enlil saw the devastation and realized the grief and despair that this caused his fellow Anunnaki, so he relented. As a result, the Anunnaki helped those that survived, and they gave mankind civilization about twelve thousand years ago. Apparently, after a few thousand years, the Anunnaki decided to stop interfering in the ways of man and left. This left mankind to fend for itself, which caused civilization to temporarily take a step backward before beginning its long growth upward.

Mainstream archeologists do not refute that the texts tell this story, but they claim it is an elaborate myth. Sitchin, on the other hand, assumed the texts were historical accounts written from the perspective of technically naive individuals trying to understand the workings of a much more sophisticated society. As improbable as this theory appears to be: (1) it explains mankind's sudden emergence; (2) it explains the worldwide existence of megalithic structures; and (3) it agrees with the ancient texts; none of which can be said about the many explanations espoused by today's experts. I was not completely convinced that Sitchin was correct, but at least he did what other archeologists refused to do: instead of establishing a theory and trying to drive all the known data into it, Sitchen took the clay tablets, along with many other writings found on obelisks, pyramid walls, and burial chambers around the world, and let the ancient texts tell their story, unencumbered by academic prejudices.

By this time I was convinced there was a massive amount of scientific evidence indicating that a highly advanced civilization existed on earth before our historical era. Mankind's history is fairly well documented over the last three thousand years, and it shows a continual process of cultural growth and sophistication. However, mankind's growth before three thousand years ago is far more speculative. Because we do not have a good record of that era, mainstream science has assumed that it too was a linear progression of cultural growth and technological improvement; but, we do not know this was the case, and indeed the archeological record tells us this is not so. I decided to go on the assumption that there was an advanced society in existence on earth before ours, and I wanted to know what they believed. They may have wondered about life as we do, or they may have had far more insight into reality. If this was the case, then I wanted to understand what they believed. The question was how to find those answers.

I figured a good place to start was with the ancient texts. Although writings that we have access to today begin about five thousand years ago, many of the original stories had been passed down through untold generations before then. I began a detailed study of the sources of all the major Eastern religions in hopes of finding some clue as to their origin. I started with the Vedas and Puranas, which were supposedly the source of Hinduism, but they were so focused on dealing with the gods that it was impossible to pull out a consistent theory on reality. I simply could not relate to the Vedic and Puranic texts. Then I found the Mahabharata, which includes the Bhagavad Gita, the Upanishads, and some other texts, and it became possible to see a body of wisdom that was being passed down through the ages. Buddhism came along as a reformation of the corruption that existed in Hinduism around 600 to 500 BC. The message coming out of Buddhism was loud and clear: all man's problems were caused by selfishness; interestingly, it was also the message coming from Jesus' teachings.

My search continued, and I greatly expanded my topics of pursuit. After every new book I read, I would peruse the bibliography for other new books, order them from Amazon, and two days later they would be on my doorstep. The Internet also aided my studies in both sources and timing. Eventually I came to realize each religion had a mystic element that was much closer to the original beliefs of the religion than the present-day doctrines, and they all seemed to have a consistent theme. I wondered what the great philosophical minds thought, so I began to seek the ideas of the ancient Eastern and Western philosophers. The older the philosopher, the more interested I was, because I felt they may have had a better understanding of the ancient beliefs; Plato was particularly interesting. Since I found hypnotic regression of interest, I started investigating other psychology subjects like consciousness studies, remote sensing, afterlife experiments, and thought experiments. Ian Stevenson's studies on biology and reincarnation were particularly interesting. I got involved with ancient and medieval histories that included the numerous Knights Templar mysteries, along with the other secret societies. I even decided to look into various mystic and astrology phenomena to see if they held any truths that I could extract. Eventually I returned to the world of physics to see if I could understand how science played into all this, which was when I discovered Dr. David Bohm, the renowned quantum physicist, and his thoughts on the implicate order.

Much to my amazement, a consistent story of reality came into focus. No matter which esoteric study I pursued, everything pointed to a consistent perspective on reality. The ancients did not have a religion; they had a philosophy that was consistent with their science, culture, and spiritual beliefs. They passed their wisdom down to our ancestors, who kept much of it hidden within their secret societies when the religious organizations in the West became controlled by dangerous and intolerant fanatics. The hermetic philosophy[2] and the Emerald Tablets were remnants of a wisdom passed down from a highly sophisticated society; even the sciences are slowly confirming the doctrine to this day. The religions of the world once preached these concepts, but over time they were set aside and replaced by other doctrines the religions felt were more supportive of their concerns.

After years of research and study, I have documented a philosophy that can be described as a new or maybe re-found worldview. Thousands of years ago, this worldview was held by many, but it was lost to mankind over the millennia. This book details this view and the life we need

---

2   See Hermetic Philosophy in Suggested Reading

to live in order to aspire to it. This worldview is not religious in origin but considers the most popular theological arguments; it does not conform to mainstream science but considers many of the latest scientific discoveries; it does not follow any particular metaphysical doctrine but considers numerous metaphysical theories; and although it does not follow any particular philosophy, it incorporates various philosophic ideas.

I believe this philosophy does the following:

1. It assures us that there is a loving God who has created the cosmos to assist us in obtaining perfection, and each spirit is a part of God and is essentially a god in the making.

2. It neutralizes society's fundamental indoctrination of the competitive nature of man to achieve and collect material objects, promoting selfishness. This does not mean that we do not perform at our maximum potential, but we measure life by more than what we possess.

3. It stresses the importance of helping less fortunate souls without worrying about getting recognition, as the reward is in the selfless act itself.

4. It allows us to understand that there is an afterlife without heaven or hell, which eliminates the fear of Judgment Day. Additionally, injuries or diseases may harm the physical body, but they will not impact the spirit. It also reduces the trauma of the passing of a loved one because we realize they have moved on to a better place and we will have the opportunity to rejoin them in the afterlife.

5. It reduces the feeling of despair when faced with life's trials, as the philosophy helps us recognize that life's issues are for our own benefit and are within our power to resolve.

6. It recognizes that all humans provide a unique and valuable perspective and are equal regardless of ethnicity, political status, employment position, education, or wealth.

INTRODUCTION

Truth is common to science, religion, and philosophy. Until we have a consistent view of the world that crosses all disciplines, we will not know truth. The beauty of truth is that it sets us free from our fears, frustrations, and helpless feelings of inadequacy. It allows us to see how we fit into this world and see the path that we are on. It lets us realize the incredible beings that we are and the infinite future that we have. Most importantly, it shows us that we are really in control of our lives. We are not at the mercy of the powers that be; we are able to change our circumstances and improve our lives by simply making other decisions. We are the masters of our destinies! I hope you enjoy the book.

CHAPTER 1

The Universal Consciousness

Spoke to me again, the Seven, saying:
From far beyond time are WE, come, O man, Traveled
WE from beyond SPACE-TIME, aye, from the place
of Infinity's end. When ye and all of thy brethren were
formless, formed forth were WE from the order of
ALL. Not as men are WE, though once WE, too, were
as men. Out of the Great Void were WE formed forth
in order by LAW. For know ye that which is formed
truly is formless, having form only to thine eyes.

– The Emerald Tablets

Key Concept:	*The Universal Consciousness (God) is a mind, and everything in existence, including us, is part of it.*

PRIMORDIAL SOUP

The ancient mystic wisdom tells us that space—including what is inside and outside the cosmos and sometimes referred to as the primordial soup or the endless void—had existed throughout eternity in a chaotic state without organization or form. It says that each subatomic element, which we

1

call matter, within this space had a conscious aspect to it. This substance, the mystics tell us, was the "father-mother" of the ancient Trinity, or what is known in Sanskrit as the Svabhâvat. It contained the building blocks of all things, including the essence of both material and spiritual elements. At a point in time eons ago, these spiritual elements came together and created a being that was known as the Son or the One in the ancient Trinity. The One had no form, as it was only spiritual energy, and its nature was that of a mind, which eventually became self-aware. Over time the One, or Being, began to understand truth and became wiser. As it grew, it realized that it had the ability to differentiate itself by dividing into separate beings or spirits. These spirits were also minds, in that they had no physical bodies but were also self-aware. They could think and act autonomously but were still connected to and part of the One. When the new entities came into being, they had the spiritual essence of the One and were collectively known in the ancient Trinity as the Holy Ghost. They also had all the innate characteristics and capabilities of the One, except they were all ignorant when they started their existence. Because the spirits had free will and ignorance, they were self-centered and were not aligned with the interests of the One. The One realized that the only way to align these entities with his wishes was to teach them the error of their selfish ways. Over time, the spirits began to understand that true contentment was helping each other and learning new things. New spirits continued to be created, and over the eons of time, this group of spirits eventually became very wise and very large, and they became known as the Universal Consciousness.

The accuracy of this ancient story is debatable, but the fact that the Universal Consciousness exists today is hard to ignore.

THE UNIVERSAL CONSCIOUSNESS

The material cosmos in which we exist is transcended by the Universal Consciousness, of which every living entity within it is a part. It is a single spiritual entity that seems to have come into existence quite by accident, but that is where the accidents stopped. We may consider the initial entity to be God, although the term God may better apply to the entire Universal Consciousness, as it has a single purpose, a single intelligence, and a single goal, and it encompasses everything in the spiritual realm, which includes our cosmos. In short:

The Universal Consciousness is a mind consisting of a single system of thought made up of an infinite number of individual units of consciousness or spirits, all working toward the single goal of perfect understanding while embracing the guiding emotional principle of pure love toward all beings.

ASPECTS OF THE UNIVERSAL CONSCIOUSNESS

Although trying to explain the Universal Consciousness runs the risk of falsely limiting it, there are a few characteristics that we can safely apply:

- Its fundamental unit is a spirit that has two aspects: (1) self and (2) soul. The self is self-aware, emotional, rational, and willful. The soul has wisdom collected from experiences, and the resulting entity is a mind.

- Because it is a mind, ideas are the only things that it values.

- It consists of vibratory energy.

- It is very real.

- It has no inherent form but takes the form of any vessel that it inhabits.

- It is immortal. Although it had a beginning, once created, it will exist forever, as there is nothing to cause it to go out of existence.

- Although it began existence as a very small entity, after an untold amount of time, this spiritual being has grown to an unfathomable size and intelligence.

- The Universal Consciousness is not localized to a specific place, like heaven, but is ubiquitous in that it is everywhere throughout the cosmos and resides in every object simultaneously[3].

- It is infinite in its capacity to learn and to create. We live in a finite spatial world, so it is difficult for us to imagine anything that is infinite in scope, but the Universal Consciousness is a mind that has no limits. It can grow to any capacity simply by gaining wisdom and understanding.

- Its thoughts are the forces that drive our cosmos. It knows all, sees all, and controls all.

- It is somehow able to divide its core spiritual element, the self[4], into an unlimited number of discrete entities, but these entities remain eternally tied to the Universal Consciousness. When a spirit is created, it is like a seed ready for growth. These spiritual seedlings always remain an integral part of and attached to the One original spirit. They grow independently but remain in communication with each other forever. It is like a sophisticated computer network where each terminal (a conscious unit) can act either independently or as a single processing system. As such, the Universal Consciousness can be viewed as many separate elements or as a single entity.

THE WAY OF THE UNIVERSAL CONSCIOUSNESS

When it came into being, it was totally ignorant. At some point it decided upon a self-directed course of learning, on which it continues to this day.

---

3   This is discussed in greater detail in chapter 6: The Illusion.

4   See chapter 3: Who We Are for more detail.

It is as close to perfect as we can conceive, yet it ever strives for further perfection. If we knew more about this entity, we would surely think that it was all wise, all knowing, all loving, all-powerful, and all willful. But because it continuously improves and perfects itself, it is always changing and strengthening its attributes.

Its goal is perfection, which it obtains through the creation and accumulation of truth. As such, it measures growth and maturity by a spirit's level of understanding.

It is all just. It has established a system of cause and effect[5] in which every spirit gets what it deserves. It never judges other spirits, no matter what they do.

It has emotions, and like us, it wants to feel good. Long ago it realized that jealousy, rage, anger, hate, and the like were negative emotions that disturbed its existence. The best feeling of all was simply blissful contentment, which it has achieved. This was attained by loving and caring for all its entities. This means that not only does it love others, but in so doing it loves itself. As such, the Universal Consciousness's feeling is unqualified love for all of its creatures, no matter how foolish and despicable they act.

Its motivation is to assist other spirits to gain wisdom and become more loving. It ensures all spirits pursue a path of growth, which it does by providing an environment that allows each spirit to follow a unique, self-directed path toward obtaining understanding and love. But like any good teacher, it establishes rules that all spirits must follow. These rules are the spiritual laws that govern the universe and are for the benefit of all. Because it loves all beings, it has only their best interests at heart.

It enjoys creation. The diverseness of the cosmos is due to the creative energies and inclination of the Universal Consciousness. Creation provides both entertainment and utility.

---

5 See chapter 4: Death and Life.

WHAT THE UNIVERSAL CONSCIOUSNESS IS NOT

The Universal Consciousness is not the humanistic God associated with the Abrahamic religions or the old Vedic scriptures per se. It never walked on this earth as a deity. It never killed anybody out of anger, and it never got reasoned out of doing something that it wanted to do. The atrocious actions that were attributed to God in the Torah and Old Testament simply are not true. These deeds may have occurred, but the Universal Consciousness was not the perpetrator.

The Universal Consciousness has no need to be glorified or praised. It has outgrown all of the self-limiting human insecurities like vanity, pride, greed, revenge, fear, etc., that make life so difficult for us. It has rid itself of all selfish motivations in its drive toward perfection. Praising God is to no avail. Our everyday thoughts and actions demonstrate our love for God, not our adoration.

The Universal Consciousness does not hand out assistance or favors to the faithful. In fact, each conscious unit is treated equally and fairly at all times, no matter what it has done. Although it is not impersonal by any means, the Universal Consciousness has established a methodology via spiritual laws whereby immature spirits are taught right from wrong and truth from falsehood. It knows what each conscious unit needs for growth and when it needs it. In turn, it provides all that is needed in a timely manner. No spirit needs to ask for help, or indeed ask for anything, because the Universal Consciousness knows best and provides everything that is needed long before it could ever be requested, as all our needs are always appropriately provided for before we need them.

The Universal Consciousness never throws anyone into hell or purgatory for eternity or even an instant. It is all loving and only has the best interests of all conscious units at heart.

SPIRITUAL REALMS

In order to control the process of spiritual growth, the Universal Consciousness created multiple levels or realms for spirits to exist and work in, depending on their level of wisdom. A realm is created out of need, and its purpose is to provide specific learning environments that cater to the most immediate deficiencies of a large group of spirits.

Each realm emanates out of a higher or wiser realm. The lower realms are supervised and controlled by the realms above them. Each aspect of a realm corresponds to an aspect in the higher realm, only in a less perfect manner. In reality there is no such thing as higher and lower realms, because each realm provides what is needed for those spirits within it to grow, and all conscious units will eventually end up in the same realm. Higher only refers to greater understanding. Our cosmos is the natural realm, and it is one of those levels.

Each realm has its own laws, which correspond to the laws on the higher realms but are finely tuned for the needs of each particular realm. We can regard the spiritual laws more like the laws of physics than our man-made laws, because they cannot be broken. The Universal Consciousness could choose to change the laws, but if a law is in place, all spirits are subject to it.

THE COSMOS

Our universe or cosmos was created and is now controlled by the combined thoughts of spirits within the Universal Consciousness. It is referred to as the material universe or natural realm. The natural realm is a manifestation of the divine's nature and emanates from the Universal Consciousness.

The natural realm was created in such a way that objects are formed by having material substances enfold around spiritual beings. When viewed through our senses, this creates the perception that the cosmos is comprised of material objects, but in actuality the cosmos consists of spiritual objects disguised as material objects. Our brains in conjunction with our senses create this illusory environment[6]. The cosmos consists of spiritual entities embedded in matter. Since all spirits are part and parcel of the One, it follows that everything that exists in the natural realm is part of the Universal Consciousness; everything!

The natural realm is a single, living, spiritually controlled organism! It is the creation of a mind that transcends space and time and yet somehow lives within it. The whole cosmos is alive and conscious and consists of virtually an infinite number of unique units of consciousness all tied together in a single system of thought. Knowledge and wisdom are shared freely and instantaneously by all beings in the spiritual realm. However, without the proper foundation, a spirit cannot understand many of the lessons of life. It would be like trying to explain the details of the theory of relativity to a person that has not learned how to add yet. As such, spiritual growth requires the continuous expansion of knowledge and wisdom as the spirit's foundation grows.

Spiritual Growth

The ancients taught that the cosmos consists of five categories of spiritual beings:

	Spirits	Elements	Included Elements
1	Superhuman	Ether-Light-Spirit	2, 3, 4 and 5
2	Man	Air-Gas-Intellect	3, 4 and 5
3	Animals	Fire-Energy-Soul	4 and 5
4	Plants	Liquid-Generation	5
5	Stones	Gems-Rocks-Earth	

Spiritual Beings in the Cosmos
Table I

---

6   See chapter 6: Illusion for more detail.

Each category in Table I consists of all the elements of the category below it plus the added characteristics listed next to it.

Everywhere we look on this earth we see life, and life cannot exist without a spiritual entity within it. Although plants and stones are alive, a single conscious unit is not necessarily dedicated to every plant and stone. Instead, each object has a spiritual entity behind it that guides its growth. In time these group souls will also climb the ladder of consciousness just like we did. Stone, vegetable, animal, and man are all just different stages of spiritual evolution. A stone is becoming a vegetable. A vegetable is becoming an animal. An animal is becoming a human, and a human is becoming a superhuman. Even the earth and stars have spiritual entities of some sort attached to them. Life is not defined by having a material body, but by having a spiritual element that resides within.

Man is a generic term for beings at a certain level of growth. Man exists throughout the cosmos and is not defined by his physical characteristics; man is defined by his spiritual maturity. Although there are many humanoid civilizations spread across the universe that we might categorize as mankind because of their appearances and lifestyles, there are many that we would not even though they are at our level of development. In fact, there are several life forms on this earth, such as whales and dolphins, that are not very different from man on an evolutionary scale.

The purpose of the universe is to provide spirits with a learning environment. We are not interlopers; the cosmos was created for us and our needs. The cosmos is always changing because as we evolve and move to higher levels, our world needs to go there with us; all things that exist in nature exist for the sake of man and the spirits that will follow him.

COSMIC CYCLES

Creation is done through the process of cycles. A cosmos is created, exists through expansion and contraction, and is then destroyed. After destruction, a long pause of inaction takes place, and then a new cosmos is created. Each period consisting of a creation, existence, destruction, and ensuing rest is known as a cosmic cycle.

In each cycle, new spiritual seedlings are released into the universe and allowed to grow. Spirits that were released and grew in previous cycles are highly advanced compared to the seedling spirits in following cycles, so they have responsibilities to aid the new spirits' growth. This not only helps the new spirits, but also helps the older spirits continue to grow, as wisdom and understanding are never-ending pursuits.

Cycles are extremely long. Some ancient mystics believed that a cycle lasted about four trillion years, whereas scientists believe our present cosmos is only about thirteen billion years old. If these numbers are even broadly correct, which is reasonable since the universe is still in the expansion stage, then we are in the beginning of this cycle. After each half cycle, everything rests for an equally long period. During the period of rest, nothing moves, nothing thinks, but nothing dies either. When this period of "night" is over, it all starts again.

Spirits retain their identities from the cycle that they were first released into. This provides a general indication of their wisdom and maturity. Although some spirits learn more quickly than others, it would be difficult to catch up to a spirit in a previous cycle because of the immense length of time it had to amass wisdom. A spirit from cycle nine would be very much wiser than one from cycle four.

GOD[7]

The Universal Consciousness is God. Unlike the humanistic descriptions of God in the various Abrahamic or Vedic texts, God is our father and is all loving. Everything described in the following chapters is a result of the laws that God put into place in order to create the kind of spiritual realm he wants. His aspirations are what we follow.

---

7   God is referred to here in the masculine; however, he is genderless.

CHAPTER 2

WHO WE ARE

Man is a star bound to a body until in the end, he is freed through his strife. Only by struggle and toiling thy utmost shall the star within thee bloom out in new life. He who knows the commencement of all things, free is his star from the realm of night.

Remember, O man, that all which exists is only another form of that which exists not. Everything that has being is passing into yet other being and thou thyself are not an exception

– The Emerald Tablets

Key Concept: *We are all gods in the making and on a journey to perfect our spirits.*

SPIRIT, SELF, AND SOUL

We are each a spiritual being having a life experience. We are unique units of consciousness within the Universal Consciousness. We have each lived many lives and died many deaths; we are immortal. Over time we will each bring a valuable perspective to the overall wisdom of the universe, but at this stage of our development we are still immature and just beginning to take responsibility for ourselves.

The spirit is the combination of: (1) the self, which allows us to be self-aware and part of the divine spirit; and (2) the soul, which allows us to be the unique entities that we are. A spirit is essentially a mind.

The self is the consciousness that makes us self-aware. It allows us to be. Our selves are immortal and were created untold eons ago. They each had a beginning but they have no end. The self is where our thinking and feeling reside, and it evolves over time as its attributes grow.

The self is also the divine part of our nature, which not only ties us to the Universal Consciousness but is part of the Universal Consciousness. This is a difficult concept to grasp, as we cannot conceive of how a single self can exist in multiple beings, but it does. How this works will remain a mystery to mankind until we understand the true nature of self. It helps to think of a self as being like a drop of water that goes into the ocean and becomes one with the ocean. Each drop still exists but is now part of a much larger entity; yet it still does its small part as an element of the ocean. As insignificant as a single drop may appear, if it were not for all the drops, there would be no ocean.

Every self has a soul permanently attached to it that functions as the permanent database where all our knowledge is stored. Everyone has had different experiences, learned different things, and developed different views on a multitude of subjects. The soul is where experiences and wisdom reside, so it is a critical element that makes us each unique. All of this information is stored in the soul. As a result, all souls are different.

The two spiritual aspects of self and soul are inseparable and have all the functions of a mind: desire, will, rationality, communication, creativity, and emotion. Spirits evolve over a great length of time and eventually become us. In our society, the words spirit and soul are often used interchangeably, but it is useful to understand that they refer to two separate things because it helps us understand the nature of our divinity.

When a spiritual element is released into the universe, the spirit begins to grow. Our spirits are the unique accumulation of knowledge that we have attained throughout our many existences. They are our personalities and our self-identities. Some of the products that the spirit continually builds upon during its continuous growth are understanding, justice, prudence, temperance, courage, happiness, love, will, and virtue.

Every living thing has a conscious unit or element of the Universal Consciousness at its core. The Universal Consciousness can be considered The All because the life force of everything that exists is part of it. As noted in the hermetic text, the Kybalion[8], **"The All is in all, and all is in The All."** We are each part of The All, which is the Universal Consciousness; as such, each of us is an elemental part of the Universal Consciousness and at the same time the Universal Consciousness is within us and all living things. It is worthwhile to reflect on this concept, as it really helps tie all these ideas together.

OUR BODIES

As humans, we can think of ourselves as being a triad that consists of a self, a soul, and a body. Our bodies are not us, although they appear to be. Our bodies are vessels that act as temporary places for our spirits to reside in order to experience life in the natural realm. The body is simply a vehicle for us to use and then discard when it has no more utility. It is like a special outfit worn for a single occasion. The clothes help us assume the role that we want to portray, like a bride and groom at their wedding. Before and after the event, they are still themselves living their daily lives. The clothes that they wear for the wedding are simply

---

8 The Kybalion is a hermetic philosophy that is purported to be the essence of the ideas of Hermes Trismesgistus, also thought to be Thoth, an Atlantian god and supposedly the author of the Emerald Tablets.

a facade that allows them and those participating with them to have a temporary experience. When the event is over, the clothes have no more value and are eventually discarded. Likewise, when this life is over, the body has no more value and is discarded.

The body acts as a home for the spirit in the natural realm. This is necessary in order to make us believe that the life we are living and the decisions that we make are crucial to our well-being. We need to take this life seriously so we can learn the most from our experiences. If we viewed life as a movie, we might be frightened or happy, but we would never be as emotionally impacted as we are playing the role for real. If we were spectators, the lessons that we are here to learn would be much more difficult to grasp and the subtleties impossible to comprehend.

The brain is the interface between the spirit and the five sense organs. It has no inherent emotion or understanding or rationality. It is a highly sophisticated device that only acts as a pathway from the senses to the mind. The brain translates the sensory data into an idea or image for our minds to interpret. When we get old and forgetful, it is only the neural paths in the brain that become less reliable, not our minds, which have all our knowledge readily available. When a person is in a coma, the mind remains aware but the interface with the world is interrupted. When the brain becomes so dysfunctional that it can no longer perform its function in a satisfactory way, the spirit will choose to leave the body and return to the spiritual realm[9].

Manly P. Hall[10] says that the ancient wisdom identified seven auric bodies or zones outside our physical bodies. These are part of us but are not material, so they remain with us at least for a while after death. A number of studies like those reported by Lynne McTaggart in *The*

---

9   See chapter 4: Death and Life for more on realms.

10 Manly P. Hall lived from 1901-1990, and spent his adult life in Los Angeles, CA, where he was a philosopher, writer, and mystic. He spent his life accumulating ancient manuscripts and writing about their meaning. His best known book was "The Secret Teachings of All Ages".

Field, seem to substantiate the fact that our bodies extend beyond the boundaries of our skin. These bodies apparently each have a color and extend four to six feet around us, which may help explain how we can sometimes sense when people are behind us without actually seeing or hearing them. Our every thought significantly impacts these bodies, just as they impact our physical bodies. Like the spirit, the body also has products like beauty, health, and the senses.

OUR SPIRITUAL ESSENCE

Inherent Aspects of Our Spirits

Our spiritual nature consists of the following six highly integrated attributes[11]: (1) desire, (2) will, (3) reason, (4) emotion, (5) imagination (creativity), and (6) communication. We use the knowledge that resides in the soul's database to make decisions, discriminate right from wrong, analyze situations, and develop understanding. The spirit is the seat of our emotions. It is happy or sad, it experiences wonder and awe, it feels love and hate, and it knows joy and sorrow. It allows us to imagine things that have never existed. It is also what drives us toward growth; it is our will and desire. Our spirit can communicate[12] with other spirits directly without the use of the brain via thought waves. In other words, our spirits are who we are.

Spirits have no gender. There are no male or female spirits. Only the material body has a gender. Spirits often change gender from one life to the next. However, if we are working a set of problems that are easiest to learn as a specific sex, we may have a bias toward that sex for several lifetimes. It is easy to see how one's sexuality might be confusing for beings that have recently changed genders after a long stint as the opposite sex. Judging others because of their sexuality only shows ignorance.

11 See Spirituality in chapter 8 for an expansion of spiritual attributes.

12 See Thought in chapter 7 for more discussion of communication.

Spirits are all equal: they have no race, no hierarchy, and no entitlements. The homeless man on the street is learning a lesson that he chose to learn just like us. Who knows, in your next life you may choose to be the homeless and he may be a king. The black slave that came over on a boat from Africa in the 1700s may be a white suburban housewife today. Every spirit has equal worth in the eyes of the Universal Consciousness.

Our spirits have existed for eons, but they never deteriorate so they always feel young and vibrant. It is only our bodies that age. This is why when we get old we don't seem old to ourselves. We may feel more aches and pains from our aging bodies, but mentally we are the same young people that we always were. Our memories, which reside in our spirit, may not seem as good, but that is only because the brain is unable to access them as well as when we were young. A spirit does not change very much over a single lifetime, and overall we are still the same people that showed up at birth, but hopefully a little wiser.

The spirit has an infinite capacity for growth. We like to say that nothing is infinite, but consciousness truly has infinite potential. It will grow forever. At some point we will each have as much power and wisdom as is contained in the entire Universal Consciousness today, but of course, by then the Universal Consciousness will be infinitely wiser than it is presently. We will never fully catch up, but we will learn to be a part of it and share in its wisdom.

Clones are not allowed in the spiritual realm. Creating unique spirits is a fundamental spiritual law. Physical clones are allowed in the natural realm, as the incarnating conscious unit is the true differentiating entity.

We are each unique because no other entity has had or will ever have the exact same experiences that we have, and our experiences and the knowledge and wisdom that we have gained from them are what make us who we are. Everyone is unique!

A spirit has free will, so it is capable of deciding what it wants to think and do. It can act in accordance with the wishes of the Universal Consciousness, or it can act separately; however, it must live within the spiritual laws, which means that if we go against the Universal Consciousness, there will be a resulting negative effect with which we will have to live.

Resonance

Like everything in the universe, a spirit consists of vibratory energies. As such, we respond to external vibrations when they correspond to the various vibrations that resonate within us. Energy from the universe continuously flows through us, but it only impacts us when our particular energy patterns are sympathetic to the vibrations. We are like vibratory tuning forks, and we each respond to certain frequencies. Music is a good example: some tunes resonate with us to the point of almost feeling magical, yet other tunes are simply annoying noise. Paracelsus, the sixteenth-century Renaissance man, said that our vibratory sympathies make it almost impossible for us not to be affected by anything that we are like and almost impossible for us to be affected by anything that we are not like. Every material object has a unique set of resonant frequencies. If we see something that appeals to us, it is because its resonant frequency is somehow sympathetic with ours.

Not only do spirits have unique energy patterns, groups of spirits also have unique signatures. Nations, religions, businesses, sports, etc., all have their own peculiar vibratory patterns or thought systems. When a group is composed of individuals with similar energy patterns, they are able to reinforce each other with unusually positive or negative results.

Sculptors, painters, architects, etc., create designs that are individual and easily identified with them. This is because we each create objects that are compatible with our energy patterns. Each of us has a certain feeling of affinity or aversion to these creations, depending on our vibratory patterns. We instinctively select the world frequencies we want to receive and surround ourselves with those items or people. This is why a person's own little world is so tuned to that person's specific needs. If we try to be people that we are not or do things with which we are uncomfortable, then we find ourselves feeling out of place. We can choose to adapt to the foreign environments if we believe they are in our best interests or return to more familiar places.

Each idea or piece of knowledge is energy[13] and constantly radiates a specific hue and brightness. A spirit is the summation of its knowledge and is simply energy vibrating at many different frequencies.

Spirits can be seen in the spiritual realm, but we are unable to see them in the natural realm because the frequency sensitivity of our eyes cannot pick up the spiritual vibrations. In our world, white light is a combination of all the other light energies that make up the visible spectrum. Similarly, the look of a spirit is simply a combination of all the colors and intensities that emanate from the spirit's knowledge; the greater the wisdom, the brighter the light. Although the self and soul each have a certain look, it pales in comparison with the spirit's knowledge. As such, a very wise being appears to a less advanced being as a bright light source.

The thought waves created from a spirit's radiating knowledge can only be perceived or picked up by those of similar or higher wisdom. A wise spirit might be invisible to those spirits that are at a lower level unless it chooses to think at an appropriate lower level. It is much like a radio that is tuned to a certain frequency. The antenna and receiver are exposed to all the frequencies around them, but they can only interpret the energy that is compatible with their system, and they are completely oblivious to any signals outside their reception bands; spirits work the same way.

---

13 See chapter 7: Thought.

Our Nature

Mind

A spirit is essentially a mind comprised completely of its thoughts. It has no other function or capability besides the abilities that comprise thinking and feeling.

We are the culmination of everything that we have ever thought. The kabbalah[14] is a Jewish mystic science that spells out a word unique to each person. The secret to the kabbalah is that our lives are that word, which is another way of saying that our lives are our thoughts. We bring upon ourselves whatever is in those thoughts. In other words, we are what we think. Like everything mental, thoughts are our only product, and our thoughts come from our experiences.

Subconscious

What we call our subconscious is really the part of the soul that cannot be directly accessed through the brain. Our past experiences and knowledge gained in previous lives are retained in the subconscious mind. Although our minds are continually being trained and retrained, they follow what they have been trained to do because the spirit always tries to do what is best for the body. However, it is not always right. Like the conscious mind, the subconscious can be misinformed if it has drawn inaccurate conclusions from past experiences. For example, if a person is habitually overweight, it may be because the spirit believes that it is in the body's best interest to be heavy. Maybe the spirit starved to death in an earlier life and it is storing up excess calories to prevent that from happening again. If we want to change that thinking, we need to retrain the spirit to understand that being overweight is not in this

---

14 The kabbalah is an ancient Jewish mystical tradition based on an esoteric interpretation of the Torah.

body's best interest[15]. The spirit can also cause the body to get sick and conversely to be healed. For example, if the subconscious believes that creating cancer cells is best for the body, then that is what it will do. In the same way, the spirit can be retrained to act differently and indeed cure the body of disease. Compared to our conscious minds, our subconscious minds have great wisdom, and it is always wise to go with our internal feelings when we are undecided.

Ignorance

Our natures are divine, not sinful. There is no such thing as a spirit having original sin[16] or any other kind of sin. It is simply an erroneous concept. Each spirit has an element of the divine self within it, so it would be impossible to be sinful without the Universal Consciousness also being sinful. The confusion occurs when ignorance is mistaken for sin. Original ignorance is ubiquitous, but no one is ever punished for what they do not know. Our mistakes have consequences that eventually teach us the errors of our ways so our ignorance slowly turns into wisdom. We are not sinful beings, just ignorant.

Stress

We live lives filled with stress, but it does not need to be that way. Life is stressful because we allow it to be so, not because it is an inherent part of our nature. We need to develop the self-confidence to know we have the capability to carry any burden we find ourselves under. The answers to all our problems can be found within our own minds because

---

15 This has been successfully accomplished many times by means of hypnotic regressions into a past life in which the problem occurred. Once the bad experience is brought to the conscious mind's attention, it can correct the misunderstandings and the problem often goes away as the subconscious mind realizes that this was a unique occurrence and it stops trying to add weight. This has also worked for other fears like panic attacks and various phobias in which a unique experience hidden within the subconscious mind negatively influences present behavior.

16 See chapter 9: Religion for an expansion on this point.

the Universal Consciousness has ensured that we have been given all the necessary tools to successfully resolve every circumstance in which we find ourselves. We cannot avoid participating in life's many crises, but if we accept them for what they are, learning experiences, then they will become much easier to handle.

Divinity

Our divine nature is guided by a preexisting and transcendent harmony that assures us of always eventually achieving our goals. The answers to many of life's deepest mysteries lie right before our eyes, and self-analysis and introspection are where to find them. The concept of looking inward to learn the answers to life's questions is not new. Socrates said that the proper study of mankind is man himself, and above the doors of an ancient Egyptian temple an inscription reads: "Man, know thyself."

Significance

Each of us is a spark in the flame of the Universal Consciousness, where we are all learning to become full-fledged members of that spiritual community. As the complexity of our entities grow, so do our opportunities to learn, and we gradually become ever more sophisticated beings. The more capable we become, the more experiences we are able to have, the more knowledge we acquire, the more that is expected of us, and most importantly, the more we expect from ourselves. We are far more important in the greater scheme of things than we appear to be.

Microcosm

Mankind is truly a microcosm of the Universal Consciousness. The Bible says we were created in God's image, but it is the spiritual image, not the humanoid image, that is like God. The ancients compared man to a lotus blossom because, like man, the blossom continues to slowly open up, exposing more and more of its beauty until the final heart is fully exposed. Like man, the inner petals are identical to the final blossom, only not yet fully formed. Pythagoras, the brilliant sixth-century BC Greek philosopher, believed that man is a microcosm of the universe, not just because he has all the characteristics and is made of the same elements, but because he has all the power of the universe within him. Both man and the cosmos are microcosms of the Universal Consciousness.

Growth

Beginning

Spirits lie dormant until they are released into the universe and allowed to grow. They start out completely ignorant, so they are put in positions to have experiences in order to begin to learn. Early on, the experiences are pretty mundane so they can learn what it feels like to simply be, and then be aware, and then be self-aware. Spirits have slow, tedious starts, but the path toward understanding is continuous.

Mistakes

The whole concept of spiritual growth is based on learning from mistakes[17]. If we did not make mistakes we would never learn the negative effects of a particular perspective. Each mistake is followed by a lesson that teaches us about the mistake. This entails seeing the problem from another view point like a victim's side of a crime. Lessons may appear to be punishment because we need to experience the effects of our actions so that we can truly appreciate their significance, but once the lesson is learned and we understand the

---

17 See chapter 6: Illusion for a more detailed discussion.

error of our ways then the mistake is forgotten and we move on to our next lesson.

Effort

Our growth and that of every other creature is driven by effort. Knowledge only comes to us by way of our actions. We need to do things and have experiences so we can appreciate the different aspects of truth. Our opinions need to be put to the test so that we can separate the false from the true. It is our nature to aspire to greater accomplishments, and it is our effort that allows it.

Power

The spirit's focus and goal is to grow by obtaining understanding through knowledge and wisdom. With wisdom comes power; not power to control others, but power to control ourselves. Understanding also provides power to create, which along with learning provides the spirit with endless entertainment, joy, and utility.

Role

Every spirit has a role to fulfill. Right now our task is to grow and become wiser, like a child in school. We help others, but our primary role is to learn. As we enter spiritual maturity, we will need to select something to do, like a first job, that will be beneficial to the Universal Consciousness and still allow us to grow. The role will be of our choosing, and we will be ready to assume the responsibility when it occurs. After we learn everything that we need to in that position, we will move on to another. Growth requires continual effort.

TRUTH, KNOWLEDGE, AND WISDOM

These three words are easily confused, so it is worthwhile defining how I am using these terms.

Truth

The information that we know is either true or false. If it is true, then it is truth, but if it is false, then it is opinion; most of what we know is opinion. Truth comes to us in stages, and until we know the complete truth, it needs to be qualified and defined within certain boundaries. For example, Sir Isaac Newton established that the law of acceleration is:

$$F = ma$$

where F is the force on an object, m is the object's mass, and a is the object's acceleration. We believed this was true for several hundred years until Albert Einstein showed that the formula only works if the velocity, v, of the object is small compared to c, the speed of light (three hundred thousand meters per second). A more accurate formula is now considered to be:

$$F = ma/(1 - v^2/c^2)^{3/2}$$

This new formula may or may not be truth, but it is at least more accurate than Newton's version; however, Newton's formula can also be considered truth, provided that it was qualified with the provision that the object must be moving slowly compared to light. As such, discovering truth is like peeling an onion; things we think are true may only be true in the context of the environment in which we are viewing them.

In the natural realm, truth is a lot harder to identify than what meets the eye, because truth is what is real, not what appears to be real. In this world of illusion[18], it is extremely difficult to separate truth from opinion.

---

18 See chapter 6: Illusions for more detail.

Knowledge

Knowledge is the ability to take aspects of the truth that we know, consider the necessary qualifications that we are aware of, and apply this to aspects of the environment. For example, if we knew the mass of an object and its velocity, we would have the knowledge to determine the needed force to cause the object to reach a certain acceleration. In other words, knowledge allows us to understand the environment around us but not to understand the conditions of the beings within it.

Wisdom

Wisdom is knowing truth as it pertains to the emotional aspects of other spirits. Wisdom allows us to know how we or other spirits will act in certain circumstances. It is not so much knowing what someone will do in a given circumstance as why they will do it. The truth needed to attain wisdom is a much higher level of consciousness than what is needed to acquire knowledge.

STATES OF CONSCIOUSNESS

Spirits are in specific states or conditions, depending on their wisdom. A spirit is not in a specific location because space and time do not exist in the higher spiritual realms. Instead we are in various states of consciousness. There are probably as many discrete states as there are spirits.

Spiritual growth changes our vibratory level in a way that allows us to receive higher-level energies. The condition of our spirit is altered by wisdom, and as such, growth is measured by a change of state.

The following is a list of broad categories of the hierarchical states of consciousness:

1. **Being:** The lowest form of existence.

2. **Awareness:** The ability to recognize that there is an external environment.

3. **Self-Awareness:** The ability to recognize one's existence within the environment.

4. **Truth vs. Opinion:** The ability to separate true from false (opinion).

5. **Knowledge:** The ability to use elements of truth to evaluate the environment.

6. **Wisdom:** The ability to use truth to evaluate emotional situations.

7. **Understanding:** The ability to know why truth is as it is.

8. **Illumination:** The ability to realize all existing truths.

9. **Projection:** The ability to radiate truth and emanate truth (i.e., build a new realm).

10. **Creation:** The ability to bring about new truths.

Human spirits in the natural realm live in a state of opinion and are working toward gaining knowledge and wisdom. Understanding is beyond our present cycle of consciousness.

OUR UNIQUE CHOICES

It is vitally important to realize that we are responsible for everything that happens to us; we caused all our problems and all our good fortune.

Self-Created Circumstances

We are who we are and we are where we are because of the decisions that we have made along our journeys, starting at the very beginning. If we are unhappy with our present lives, then the onus is on us to change them by doing things differently. Nobody is forcing us to live this life this way. Our lives are reflections of continual streams of self-created circumstances. We cannot blame our problems on others. If we want to know who caused all our problems, then we need to look no farther than the nearest mirror. On the other hand, if we are happy with ourselves and life seems to be working well for us, then we should take heed, as we must be doing something right.

Limitations

All our limitations are self-imposed. How many times have we told ourselves that we cannot do something because of outside influences? We justify our actions because we see ourselves as helpless victims manipulated by circumstances beyond our control. Admittedly, we may have to learn how to accomplish our new tasks, but that is well within our power. No one is stopping us from doing anything. We may need to change our priorities and do a good bit of research, but most of all we need to change our outlooks to can-do attitudes. Many of us are convinced that life has given us bad breaks, so we believe that everything bad that has happened to us was someone else's fault, maybe even fate. We need to realize that all of our problems are self-generated. Dwelling on the negative attracts these problems to us. We have no limits except the ones that are self-imposed.

OUR JOURNEY OF PERFECTION

Ubiquitous

Each of us is a member of a ubiquitous spiritual community that inhabits not only this earth and other worlds like it, but indeed the entire cosmos and all the spiritual realms. Even though our relatives and friends are some of the spirits we work most closely with life after life, the people living in squalor in the third world countries or those living under totalitarian rule in, say, the Middle East or Africa are as much our spiritual family as are our blood siblings. The spirits that have incarnated into humans on this earth are all very close together in their spiritual maturity; some are just arriving and some are about to leave, but we are all at roughly the same level. We are all part of a single group that we call humanity or mankind, and we are all working together, united in a common cause.

Not Alone

We are not alone; the entire universe is teeming with life. Life is everywhere. As we explore the ocean depths and the far reaches of the galaxy, we will begin to understand that life exists throughout the cosmos. Life ranges from single-celled animals to life forms so advanced that they rival parts of the spiritual realm. We are all on a path of growth, and all life, no matter what incarnation it has taken, is part of mankind. A catastrophe felt anywhere in the world, or even anywhere in the universe, is felt by all of us. John Donne could not have been more right when he said: "Send not to know for whom the bell tolls, it tolls for thee."

Individual Journey

Each spirit is on a personal journey of growth. Growth is defined as increasing our understanding of the way things are and becoming a better person. Spirits are immortal and need a focus to keep them headed in the right direction through all of eternity. The Universal Consciousness has decided that there is no better path for every spirit than the perfection of its soul.

Our journeys are self-directed. We are responsible for what we learn, when we learn it, and if we learn it. Although we have a great deal of divine support, it is our responsibility to put in the effort and learn the lessons. Our free will allows us to do what we want, when we want, but each choice has a consequence we have to live with. We soon learn that bad decisions have bad effects and good decisions have good effects. Nature teaches us right from wrong, but we decide which path to take and how long to stay on it. The urgency and direction of our journey is at our discretion. The only thing that we cannot do is end the journey; pause and rest, yes, but end it, no.

It is a journey of personal responsibility. We and only we are responsible for our own development, and correspondingly, we are not responsible for anyone else. Although the decisions others make are not our responsibility, it is our responsibility to assist others where we can. Helping others along the way also helps us as well.

No two journeys are identical. Every being is of equal value, but each of us is at a slightly different point on the journey; not necessarily further along, just in a different place. The journey isn't straight but it is always forward. Every spirit has its own experiences and its own understanding of those experiences. As such, we each develop our own perspective on truth. The uniqueness of each individual spirit's viewpoint is what gives it a special value to the whole.

Nature of Truth

The ancients tell us that the perfection of the soul is the pursuit of truth. In desire, truth is aspiration. In action, truth is virtue. In reason, truth is wisdom and understanding. In feeling, truth is love. In creation, truth is beauty. In communication, truth is completeness. Manly P. Hall tells us, and I paraphrase, *truth is an ever-evidenced sufficiency. It is absolute reason, absolute security, and transcendent completeness. In everything that is, there is a certain evidence of adequate purpose.* Truth is the way things are and the way things should be. We live in a world of opinions, and few of them are true. Knowing what is false is as important as knowing what is true. Truth will allow us to understand the cosmos and everything in it. As we learn to see the world as it really is, treat others better than we treat ourselves, and appreciate the creations that surround us, we will rise ever higher through the states of existence.

Truth is ever evolving, as the Universal Consciousness continuously gains in understanding and creates new truth; truth has no final state. Although we seek truth, we will never fully find it because it is always coming into being; it is ever expanding. But we can certainly gain a great deal of understanding about it as we continue to evolve. Probably the best way to pursue truth is to aspire to seek virtue, wisdom, love, and beauty in everything that we do to the best of our abilities.

Our Purpose

We have chosen this life because it best helps us learn certain lessons. We cannot understand some concepts until we have established stronger bases of knowledge from which to work. In order to comprehend some of the most important truths, we need to establish better foundations to build upon. As such, our paths may seem circuitous, but every lesson has a purpose, every experience has a meaning, and patience is required, as every idea has its time.

As we gain knowledge and wisdom, our actions become more benevolent, kinder, more understanding, and more helpful. We show more tolerance for others, care less about competing against others, and care more about competing against ourselves. We care less about the physical world and its trappings. Ideas become more important than material things. Helping others find their way becomes more satisfying than wishing them failure in hopes of making us look better in comparison. We more willingly accept personal responsibility for our actions instead of blaming others. The treadmill of life becomes less important. Life begins to make sense and becomes more enjoyable and meaningful.

The Eastern religions tell us that the goal in life is to escape the cycle of life and death, but this is misguided, as it is just these cycles that allow us to evolve. The goal is not to escape life's experiences but to escape the stress of these experiences. We need to embrace our mistakes, live lives of virtue, and enjoy the journey. When we become too wise to be men, then we become light beings, and other challenges will await us. Perfection of our souls requires pursuing God's ever-evolving truths, using effort and personal responsibility as our means, and relying on our spiritual nature for our tools.

Life has a purpose, we have a purpose, the cosmos has a purpose, and indeed everything in existence, include our most obscure thoughts, has a purpose. The purpose of everything is the pursuit of perfection.

We need to aspire to be the most perfect spirits that God ever created!

CHAPTER 3

REINCARNATION

Steadily upward throughout the ages, growing,
expanding into yet another flame,
lighting the darkness with yet greater power,
quenched yet unquenched by the veil of the night.

So grows the soul of man ever upward,
quenched yet unquenched by the darkness of night.

– The Emerald Tablets

Key Concept:	***There is strong medical and scientific evidence supporting reincarnation.***

REINCARNATION: THE ESSENTIAL ELEMENT FOR SPIRITUAL EVOLUTION

Incarnation is the process that allows our spirits to integrate into organic bodies and appear to be at one with them. This is a necessary deception that allows us to believe the bodies we join are truly us. The process of a spirit incarnating over and over again is referred to as reincarnation. This is one of the most difficult concepts for many Westerners to accept, even though over 50 percent of the world's population accepts it and indeed takes it for granted. The key issues confronting Westerners are: (1) a cultural bias against it, and (2) the lack of memory of previous lives. Unfortunately, the campaign of negativity and ridicule that has been successfully waged against reincarnation by the religious hierarchies and supported by many scientists throughout the last fifteen hundred years has taken its toll on reincarnation's acceptance. However, when we understand the roots of this bias and see the extensive supporting evidence, it becomes much easier to open our minds to the concept.

The fear of incarnation into a nonhuman body is probably the biggest concern voiced by nonbelievers. People have been taught that they could reincarnate as a cow or some other lower form of life, but the spirit has been there and done that and learned those lessons, so there would be no reason to go back. The true doctrine of reincarnation says that we must incarnate into an equal or higher life form, and it is impossible to go backward. Our journey is to grow, and the universe is on a one-way path forward. No human comes back as a cow no matter what some Hindu priest might say.

UNDERSTANDING REINCARNATION

There are many reasons why Western religions and science have not supported reincarnation. Christianity struggles with accepting reincarnation because the Christian message has been structured such that mankind has only one life to either believe that Jesus was the son of God or be relegated to eternal hell. Mainstream Judaism and Islam do not include reincarnation in their doctrines, but neither doctrine would be seriously impacted by accepting reincarnation. In fact, both religions have strong mystic traditions that support it.

When a religion proclaims its doctrine to be the word of God rather than a rational philosophy of reality, then no conflicting rationale is considered; therefore, the Western religions will never be inclined to review this issue until it is widely accepted by their members. Western science also shuns reincarnation because: (1) it has deep cultural ties to Christianity, and (2) it is focused completely on the natural realm while totally ignoring any spiritual aspects that may be present. However, science is having a difficult time ignoring the massive amount of supporting data that continually pours in from highly reliable sources. It seems most people who have seriously investigated the scientific data supporting reincarnation, and have done so with open minds, inevitably convince themselves that reincarnation is either a fact of life or, at a minimum, realize the supporting data is too difficult to ignore. This is especially true in the last fifty years, because the exponential increase in communication has helped bring some amazing information to light. Probably the biggest handicap to the wider acceptance of reincarnation is the stigma that is still attached to it. Many people in the academic and scientific fields are concerned that their reputations and employment will be negatively impacted if they publicly support reincarnation. However, if we are looking for truth but ignoring the available data and submitting to group or peer pressures, then we are not going to find it.

PERSONAL SEARCH

When I began my search, I was equally dismissive of reincarnation because I was brought up in this opinionated culture. I had the same biases to deal with, but after evaluating numerous research efforts by individuals with apparently impeccable reputations and far more to lose than gain by coming down on the side of reincarnation, I realized that it is not only true, it is the only plausible truth. I cannot convince you in a single chapter, or even a single book, that reincarnation is true if you are dead set against it, or even highly skeptical as I once was. It took me many years of reading account after account, talking to people who had firsthand experiences, and considering the massive amount of evidence available to finally accept the reality of reincarnation. As such, if you are struggling with the subject and are committed to understanding it, then do not give up. This is a very difficult concept for Westerners to grasp because of our prejudices, but once we realize it is indeed how the world works, it opens up a whole new understanding of who we are and allows us to better see how the universe operates.

Rigorously going through all my investigations and substantiating rationale would be far too lengthy for this book; besides, a convincing argument on any subject is highly dependent on the reader's background and level of skepticism. As such, instead of trying to convince you that reincarnation is a reality, I will provide you with a sampling of the key data that helped convince me and provide you a path forward, which might assist you in your search.

MEDICAL AND PSYCHIATRIC DATA

Hypnotic Regression (HR)

Dr. Brian Weiss's book titled *Many Lives, Many Masters* is a good place to begin if you have had no experience with hypnotic regression. Dr. Weiss graduated summa cum laude from Columbia University in 1966 and received a medical degree from Yale University in 1970. He worked in the Department of Psychiatry at Yale University and then at the University of Pittsburgh; later, he became the chairman of the Department of Psychiatry at Mount Sinai Medical Center and associate professor at the University of Miami's school of medicine. In 1980 Dr. Weiss met a patient named Catherine who suffered from anxiety attacks and a broad range of fears including water, airplanes, choking, etc. After she did not respond to eighteen months of traditional therapy, Dr. Weiss decided to try hypnotic regression to see if some trauma occurred in her childhood that may have caused her fears. To both their surprise, while under hypnosis, Catherine was able to regress to previous lives. She was able to move through those lives at will, stop at important circumstances, and relate them in incredible detail. Over a several-year period and many sessions, Catherine was able to recall a dozen previous lives as well as the time between her previous lives. She was able to remember specific incidents that corresponded to each of her fears. As time progressed and she was able to bring these incidents into her conscious mind, her fears began to rapidly disappear. Eventually she was no longer plagued by these symptoms and was able to live a confident and happy life. Since that time, Dr. Weiss has explored the past lives of more than four thousand patients with similar results. It turned out to be a common occurrence for patients hypnotized by Dr. Weiss to remember past lives.

I found this nothing short of astonishing, if indeed it was true, so after reading this account I wanted to see if this phenomenon was common across other psychiatrists. I searched for other books on hypnotic regression, which were easy to find. Although there are many questionable authors who are attempting to take advantage of the subject, there are some very good authors. For example, Dr. Michael Newton found similar results with literally tens of thousands of patients around the world. One of the most startling findings for me was that under hypnosis many of the patients became fluent in languages with which they had no familiarity in this life. This is known as xenoglossy, and since the sessions were recorded and language experts were able to interpret and verify the recordings, this seemed hard to refute. I eventually sought out psychiatrists who had not written books or tried to make money on hypnotic regression yet performed similar therapy, and I found their experiences were indeed very similar. Hypnotic regression critics' main argument is that hypnosis causes patients to hallucinate, but that made little sense to me. When a hypnotized person is fluent in a language that they are unfamiliar with in their conscious state, hallucination is an irrational cause. When this is coupled with a detailed description of that language's culture that is verifiable by other means, reincarnation is a cause that needs to be seriously considered. Although it is impossible to explain these phenomena as illusions, they continue to be ignored by modern science as evidence for the concept of reincarnation.

Near-Death Experiences (NDE)

I then looked at near-death experiences (NDE) to see if they correlated with the hypnotic regression results. Dr. Raymond Moody and others have found many cases of people who were either seriously injured in accidents or went through serious operations, and were often diagnosed as clinically dead, who remembered experiences that they believed were spiritual in nature. When these accounts were taken over a large number of cases and common ideas were extracted, they compared exactly with the hypnotic regression experiences. In a nutshell, people who experienced NDEs inevitably noticed that when they died their souls left their bodies and appeared to float above them and had no feeling of attachment to them. The spirit immediately would see a small light at the end of a tunnel and was able to follow it by just thinking that it wanted to. The spirit was then greeted by loved ones that had previously passed away. Then, of course, the spirit was convinced to return to the body, or it would not be able to tell us the story. Although each account has its own peculiar aspects, almost all NDEs seem to follow this consistent pattern, which is exactly what is reported by hypnotic regression accounts of death, except the spirits do not return to their bodies.

Remembered Experiences

About the time I was beginning to take reincarnation seriously, I stumbled across Ian Stevenson's book *Where Reincarnation and Biology Intersect*, which is one of the best scientifically argued accounts in support of reincarnation that I have found. The book is an abbreviated version of Stevenson's impressive multivolume work on reincarnation. Stevenson was a medical doctor at the University of Virginia, where he headed the Department of Psychiatry and was the director of the division of personality studies. He had many scholarly papers to his credit before he began his long career in paranormal research. Stevenson devoted forty years to the scientific documentation of past-life memories of children and adults from all over the world and had over three thousand cases in his files. In many of the cases he studied, violent death had played a key part. The main thrust of his work was to establish a correlation between birthmarks and birth defects in children, and wounds caused by violent death in a supposed previous life. Most of the cases Stevenson investigated were in countries that had a wide acceptance of reincarnation, like Hindu and Buddhist countries in Asia and Shiite countries like Lebanon and Turkey. Stevenson believed that the birthmarks that corresponded to wounds caused by the deceased's death were the best indication of a spiritual connection of the two personalities, and as a result, he was especially particular about finding detailed mortuary reports.

Stevenson's approach was to investigate stories of children with past-life memories. Typically if past-life memories occurred, it was first noticed in children between two and four years old who would begin to tell their parents that they had lived before. They would often remember their previous families, and eventually, after months or years of nagging, the parents were often willing to take the children to find their remembered families. The children would often be able to guide their parents to their old house once they were in the neighborhood. Usually the children recognized some if not all of the people in the home, knew their way around the house, and offered personal information about a deceased family member that was corroborated by the family. Inevitably the remembered family member had died a year or so before the child was born. The deceased usually died suddenly and sometimes violently but often at a fairly young adult age. Occasionally Stevenson was able to find detailed mortuary records describing the deceased's death and a description of their fatal wounds, and often the wounds corresponded with birthmarks on the children. Usually the children lost their memories of the past lives by the time they were seven or eight and always lost them by the end of their teens. However, the relationship between a child and the remembered family often lasted a lifetime if the remembered family considered the child to be a reincarnated relative. By the time Stevenson found out about such incidents, months or even years might have gone by since the families had initially met. Stevenson was never present at the initial meeting, so he needed the child and members of the two families to corroborate the events. Stevenson's data seemed to imply that the deceased died before the spirit had accomplished what it wanted in its earlier life and had a driving need to return.

In another book, *Unlearned Language: New Studies in Xenoglossy*, Stevenson related his exploration of two of the most interesting and well-documented xenoglossy cases on record: Dolores Jay, who manifested under hypnosis as Gretchen, a German-speaking personality, and Uttara Haddur, a native of Maharashtra in western India, who over a fifteen-year period of her life was repeatedly taken over by the personality of Sharada, a young nineteenth-century Bengali-speaking woman. In the former case, Jay was fluent in German when under hypnosis, a language to which she was never exposed. In the latter case, Sharada was able to speak Bengali, a foreign language for her, and was able to identify many accurate details of Bengali life in the 1800s, such as various kinds of foodstuff of which she would have had no knowledge in her present life. Stevenson thoroughly researched these two accounts and was convinced they were credible.

Stevenson was a conscientious and meticulous researcher; all of his data is interesting, and much is very persuasive. However, he is no more successful than anyone else in suggesting a credible mechanism for the transfer of memories in apparent reincarnations, or in explaining how physical characteristics of a dead person could become imprinted on an unborn fetus.

Stevenson was extremely well thought of by his peers in the academic and scientific fields, and I never found an instance where his character was impugned. His major detractors said that he was probably misled by the people that he talked to or the interpreters, but none of his actual findings were ever disproved. In fact, his critics often seemed to have other motivations or biases, such as religious connections or the like. I found Stevenson's research far more convincing than the detractors' arguments, and I consider his research essential reading for anyone wondering if reincarnation is true.

Summary of Medical Evidence

1. Medical therapy has discovered many cases of prior life memory recollections among young children. These memories were studied, categorized, and confirmed through rigorous research.

2. Details that subjects recalled about their prior lives correspond to historical records. Furthermore, there was consistency among multiple people with prior life recollections of the same time periods and geographical areas.

3. Some subjects were fluent in foreign or ancient languages that they did not learn or have any exposure to during this lifetime. If hypnosis was involved with the recollection, then after the session ended the person no longer could speak or understand that language.

4. Some subjects among relatives, friends, or even strangers, recalled the same people, events, and details independently.

5. Recalling past-life agonies and events was instrumental in addressing and often alleviating today's ills and problems, such as panic attacks and other phobias.

PSYCHICS

Science has discredited psychics for years because psychics look beyond the natural world for answers; but since some psychics time and again are able to accurately explain events they had no rational way of knowing and even predict future events, then I figured in good conscience they could not be summarily dismissed.

Edgar Cayce, who was probably the most famous psychic in the twentieth century, was born on a Kentucky farm in 1877 and was an average, unassuming man. He worked as, among other things, an insurance salesman, photographer, and store owner. His hobbies were gardening and teaching Sunday school, and he was a devout Christian all his life. When he was a young adult, he and members of his family developed several serious afflictions, and even though he had no medical training, he was able to cure them by going into a self-induced meditation or trance, at which time he spoke of a successful remedy. His fame soon spread, and he began giving readings for strangers that resulted in an amazing number of cures.

After a few years he was asked to give broader readings, which included such topics as astrology, ancient civilizations, financial reports, and anything else interviewers could think to ask him. Between 1901 and 1945, Cayce gave 14,306 readings. Besides his massive number of healings, he accurately predicted such things as the 1929 stock market crash, World War II, and finding the Dead Sea Scrolls in 1945. Cayce believed that he received his information primarily from his subconscious mind, but occasionally he was able to obtain information from other spiritual sources.

He spoke of reincarnation as factual while in his trances, but he struggled with it for years during his waking hours until he was able to reconcile it with his deep Christian faith. He never accepted money for his readings and consequently was a poor man all his life. How Cayce was able to cure hundreds of people, speak foreign languages, and predict future events with no previous exposure to this knowledge is an unanswered question

THE ORIGIN OF OUR BIASES AGAINST REINCARNATION

I began to wonder why, if half the world believed in reincarnation and numerous medical and psychiatric accounts seemed to affirm it, I struggled with the concept. Like most people searching for truth, I did not take what either religion or science said to be the last word on anything; but it was interesting to realize how influential their doctrines have been on my beliefs. I was raised in a Christian family and taught from an early age that reincarnation was nonsense. I was told we had only one chance at being saved, and it was what we believed in this life that was all-important—even more important than how we lived our lives. As I matured I began to question my beliefs and found them to be completely irrational. Although over the past fifty years science continually altered its proclamations regarding the nature of reality when new information was accepted, religion remained firmly entrenched in its dogma. I eventually realized just how much baggage I continued to lug around from my childhood lessons, and it became important to me to understand where my negative views on reincarnation originated.

Christianity

The Western religions[19] are the most vocal critics of reincarnation because it usurps their power over their members and significantly weakens their creeds' rationales. It surprised me to realize that up to and well after the time of Jesus, virtually everyone accepted reincarnation as

---

19 See chapter 9: Religion.

a fundamental principle, including Jesus, as it was the prevailing belief in Hinduism, Buddhism, Judaism, and indeed, the entire known world.

Christians believed in reincarnation for the first five hundred years after Jesus, and they continued to do so until Holy Roman Emperor Justinian, who may not have even been a Christian, forced the Christian church bishops to ban reincarnation at the fifth ecumenical council circa AD 545. At the time it was a highly controversial decision and supposedly only passed by a single vote, even though Justinian dictated the result. As the doctrine was slowly canonized some five hundred to one thousand years after the death of Jesus, the church leaders followed Justinian's edict because it helped pull together the story that they wanted to tell. Slowly but surely during Christianity's evolution, Jesus' message and attempt to revise Judaism took a back seat to the personal ambitions of the church and state, and much of what Jesus taught was lost.

In *The Case For Reincarnation* Joe Fisher notes that: *"the fact remains that before Christianity became the vehicle for the imperial ambitions of Roman Emperors, rebirth was widely accepted amongst the persecuted faithful."*[20]

Fisher goes on to say: *"Believers in reincarnation were neither to be induced by promises of heavenly bliss nor intimidated by threats of hellfire; they didn't need priests and ritual devices such as the confessional to guide them along the straight and narrow path to God."*[21]

Between 1947 and 1956, a set of documents known as the Dead Sea Scrolls was found in Egypt. The documents are believed to have been written between 400 BC and AD 200. Many of the texts were copies of known Jewish and Christian documents, some of which are included in the Bible and Torah. Among these texts were documents known as the Gnostic Gospels. These writings expand on the four Gospels (Mathew, Mark, Luke, and John) canonized by the church and included in the New Testament.

---

20 Joe Fisher, *The Case for Reincarnation* page 107.

21 Joe Fisher, *The Case for Reincarnation* page 114.

Gnostic Gospels like Origin and Thomas expanded on the many sayings attributed to Jesus, including clear passages showing that Jesus believed in and taught reincarnation. Unfortunately, the church fathers decided not only to disagree with these teachings but to ban them as heretical. They destroyed or confiscated all of the copies they could find, and they went missing for fifteen hundred years until all of a sudden they turned up as part of the Dead Sea Scrolls. It seemed clear to me that any organization so driven as to ban and destroy certain books and beliefs must have a hidden agenda, and I was sure it was based on self-interest.

Although much of the support for reincarnation was kept out of the Bible during its creation and many revisions, the revisionists did not succeed in getting it all.

John 3:3[22]: "Jesus answered and said to him, 'truly, truly, I say to you, unless one is born again he cannot see the kingdom of God.' "

This "born again" has nothing to do with the modern-day practice of rededicating one's life to Christ as is thought in many fundamentalist sects. This "born again" really means to be born again *just* like it says.

John 3:8[23] "The wind blows where it wishes and you hear the sound of it, but do not know where it comes from and where it is going; so is everyone born of the spirit."

John clearly believed the spirit is alive before it is born.

It soon became apparent to me that the Christian doctrine is based on a number of false premises, and disbelief in reincarnation is a major one. It was obvious to the founders and political leaders of the time that the church would have more difficulty influencing its flock if the people believed they had multiple lives to perfect their souls. Also, the church knew the people would not need to believe Christ's self-appointed emissary, the church, was necessary to save them if God was guiding their

---

22 NASB Study Bible, page 1520.

23 NASB Study Bible page 1520.

spiritual growth through reincarnation and karma. In fact, the pope, who put himself between God and man, would lose all his self-proclaimed godly authority. Eventually I realized that reincarnation simply did not work within the confines of Christianity as it was implemented, and it had been intentionally excluded from the doctrine.

I soon began to realize that my reincarnation misgivings had no legitimate foundation, but I thought it would be interesting to see how reincarnation was addressed in the other two main Abrahamic religions: Judaism and Islam. Since all three religions had similar origins, I figured that I would find traces of a belief in reincarnation in them as well.

Judaism

The fact that reincarnation is part of the Jewish tradition will come as a surprise to many people, but it made sense to me after what I discovered with Christianity. All religions have a strong mystical element, which is purported to be the real teachings of the religion that are only known to the initiates, or those special individuals that have achieved higher learning.

As one would expect, Judaism has a very strong mystical element, which is known as the *kabbalah;* the name applies to the whole range of Jewish mystical activity. The keystone concepts of the kabbalah are written in the Zohar, which was said to be revealed more than two thousand years ago. The *Zohar* is a spiritual text that supposedly explains the secrets of the Jewish Bible, the universe, and every aspect of life. The Zohar clearly states that the concept of reincarnation is an accepted aspect of Jewish belief, as can be seen below:

> Zohar II 186b[24]: "And so long as a man is unsuccessful
> in his purpose in this world, the Holy One, blessed be
> He, uproots him and replants him over and over again."

---

24 The Zohar, Volume 2 page 212

Somewhere along the way, mainstream Judaism lost the concept of reincarnation, just like Christianity, probably in its attempt to placate the political powers of the time. Unfortunately, this made it much more difficult for Jews to understand the nature of the universe and how they fit into it.

Islam

Islam also builds the case for reincarnation, as stated in the Quran:

> Sura 71:17-18:[25] "And Allah has produced you from the earth, growing (gradually), and in the end He will return you into the (earth), and raise you forth,"
>
> Sura 2:28[26]: "How can ye reject the faith in Allah?- Seeing that ye were without life, and He gave you life; then will He cause you to die, and will again bring you to life, and again to Him ye return.",
>
> Sura 6:95[27]: "It is Allah who causeth the seed grain and the date stone to split and sprout. He causeth the living to issue from the dead, and He is the One to cause the dead to issue from the living."

Clearly the Abrahamic religions have a long history in the belief of reincarnation.

Science

Western religions are not the only cause of cultural biases against reincarnation. Science rejects reincarnation, and indeed the entire spiritual world, because it is only focused on the material world. Science has evolved over the last five hundred years from a body of knowledge

---

25 The Holy Qur'an page 1536

26 The Holy Qur'an page 23

27 The Holy Qur'an page 321

describing the great truths of its time, like alchemy and other metaphysical concepts, into an experimental methodology. This was originally done in Europe in order to combat the tyrannical forces of religion, and it has continued to this day. In an effort to divide power and responsibilities, science focused on the physical environment and left the spiritual world to religion, which in time it came to regard as fantasy.

The scientific method is a well-known process that relies on repetitive results from controlled experiments. This works well for phenomena that can be isolated from external events and contained in well-controlled environments like laboratories. However, it does not work nearly as well when the primary driving force of the experiment is outside of the controlled area, like the spiritual world.

The scientific method has greatly enhanced our understanding and use of material objects, but it has come at a price. It has caused us to temporarily lose focus of the ultimate goal of understanding reality and substituted instead a focus on manipulating our physical environment to achieve technological advances. Many of the great truths known to past civilizations have been discarded because we are not sophisticated enough to establish controlled experiments that are able to reproduce them in the laboratory.

Reincarnation falls into this category. No matter how much data points to a transcendent spiritual force or an eternal soul within each person, science clings to its dismissive notions.

Since science has not found the soul yet, it is impossible for it to see that the soul returns time and again. Instead it views life as simply a well-organized (by whom, one might ask) material body with a fantastic nervous system that somehow has become self-aware. Science believes that when the body dies there is nothing left to go on living. Even though fringe elements within science are finding amazing new discoveries supporting the independence of consciousness and the body[28], old ideas are

---

28 The suggested reading list, under "consciousness", lists several books describing how scientific experiments are indicating the existence of the soul.

hard to alter. Science will never come to grips with a true description of reality until it recognizes that the universe is the effect and not the cause.

Personal Misgivings

Many people argue against reincarnation by saying they cannot remember previous lives so how could they have lived them. Actually, many people do remember past lives, or at least parts of them, but do not like to talk about it because of fear of ridicule. The problem is that past-life memories are in the subconscious mind where we have trouble reaching them. When you have a déjà vu experience yet have no recollection of ever being in a particular place before, it is likely you have triggered a memory from a past-life experience. Hypnosis seems to consistently open a path to the subconscious; certain people with unusual psychic abilities, like Edgar Cayce, seem to be able to open paths to the subconscious at will, but the rest of us are left with only occasional glimpses into previous lives or none at all.

There are good reasons why we need to live in the cosmos and cannot remember our past lives in any great detail. *Emotional experiences are easier to learn in the natural realm,* where we can feel anxieties and pleasures, rather than in the spiritual realm, where life is safe and loving. However, if we could not get over our most dreaded experiences, we would never be able to move on to new lessons; we would be stuck in the past. Reincarnation serves a vital utilitarian need and is the key to learning, as it provides us the ability to forget our mistakes of the past[29]. It is necessary that we leave the past behind so we can experience the present. As such, the subconscious is responsible for remembering our past mistakes, and we will have access to these memories when we are in the spiritual realm, but then we will also understand the surrounding circumstances and be able to deal with them rationally.

---

29 See chapter 6: Illusions.

There is another practicality of forgetting: previous lives are blocked out of our consciousness because the spirits we work with are often the same from life to life but their roles are different in each life. For example, if you knew that your daughter in this life had been your father in a previous life, it would be difficult to live this life in a normal way. We evolve together, helping each other, and when we meet someone new that we instantly like or dislike, it is because we have worked with them before.

ASPECTS OF REINCARNATION

Philosophically speaking, reincarnation solves the problem of having an all-powerful and all-good God that allows evil not only to exist, but to appear to thrive. This conundrum all changes when reincarnation is introduced, and we only have experiences that we need to learn our lessons. A person that appears to be getting away with a crime in this life will pay for his indiscretions in another life, and an innocent victim may not be so innocent if multiple lives are considered. It is a rational solution to one of the great moral mysteries of life.

There is also no need for divine intervention, because the divine has already interceded to make sure we get only what we need and deserve. We do not need to ask for help. We just need to live a life of integrity, and when we make a mistake we need to do the right thing and own up to it.

The purpose of the cosmos is to function as a school or training ground for a multitude of souls all at different levels of consciousness. It makes little sense that we could spend fifty to a hundred years and learn all the lessons necessary to become a full-fledged adult spirit that is ready to take its place in the eternal service of the divine; and what about infants and children that die before they have a chance to grow? Is it fair that they never get a chance to mature? If they could mature in heaven, there would be no need for the cosmos. Reincarnation solves these issues; it removes heaven and hell from the equation because there is no need for punishment and reward or even judgment. It is all taken care of in our subsequent incarnations as we reward and punish ourselves in future lives. No one would purposely treat others poorly if they knew that they were going to receive that same treatment.

Maybe the most comforting aspect of reincarnation, at least for Christians, is that no souls are ever lost. Salvation is not a single act or decision by the divine; it is a long road of effort that happens eventually no matter how badly we have acted in the past. We are all saved through our efforts and right action. It may come as a surprise to some that salvation comes through effort and is not bestowed because of belief.

If personal growth is not the purpose of life, then existence has no purpose.

CONCLUSION

There is a lot more proof that reincarnation is true than our mainstream scientists and theologians are willing to admit. Although reincarnation is a difficult concept for many of us to come to grips with, it is critical to our worldviews and understanding ourselves. Just because half the world believes in reincarnation does not make it true; and likewise, just because half the world does not believe in reincarnation does not make it false. We each need to judge it on its own merits and leave our biases behind. A few things can be said about the many people that have worked with and written and talked about their personal experiences with reincarnation:

1. Many of them are reliable researchers who are well known and respected in their academic fields.

2. The information they obtained is consistent across a huge number of cases.

3. They gain nothing from fabricating their data, as publishing data supporting reincarnation will not bring them promotions or praise at work. On the contrary, publications on such a controversial subject are more likely to bring ridicule and negatively affect their careers. Also, books on reincarnation are not very popular in Western society and are not best sellers, so the motive for earning money is minimal.

4. People who believe in reincarnation feel that good is rewarded with good and bad returns bad; no believer would want to lie and cause himself future suffering.

5. Many researchers are harassed by religious extremists who feel that their beliefs are being called into question.

6. Whether their data supports or denies reincarnation, their research breaks through into a previously taboo subject matter.

Reincarnation is simply the cyclical wave of spiritual movement in and out of life for the purpose of spiritual growth! It allows us to appreciate good by experiencing the lack of it.

Anyone that is truly troubled over this principle should make it a point to fully understand it. The bibliography and suggested reading list contains a number of references that will be helpful. I encourage you not to believe what you have been told about reincarnation, but to search for the answers yourself with an open mind.

It takes time to understand reincarnation and become fully comfortable with it, because it requires us to go against a conflicting concept that has been ingrained within us. It also requires a good deal of contemplation, but over time our subconscious gut feelings tell us what is true. Everything worthwhile in life requires effort, and understanding reincarnation is no different; only those willing and ready to search will find truth.

CHAPTER 4

DEATH AND LIFE

I, Death, come, and yet I remain not,
for life eternal exists in the ALL;
only an obstacle, I in the pathway,
quick to be conquered by the infinite light.

Awaken, O flame that burns ever inward,
flame forth and conquer the veil of the night.

Then in the midst of the flames
in the darkness grew there one that
drove forth the night, flaming, expanding,
ever brighter, until at last was nothing but Light.

– The Emerald Tablets

Key Concept:	*Life is a temporary excursion into the natural realm, and death is simply a transition back to our normal spiritual state that need not be feared.*

INTRODUCTION

Death is a subject that we all talk about, but it is assumed that we cannot know anything about it until it happens to us. This may not necessarily be the case, as there are a number of fascinating accounts of people recalling their previous lives and even their existences in between lives. Literally thousands of patients working with hundreds of psychiatrists using hypnotic regression techniques around the world have provided amazing stories of their previous lives and their activities between lives. The consistency across the multitudes of accounts is remarkable considering that each person views the death experience from his or her own perspective; and especially since the results can be further skewed by the type of questioning the doctor pursues. Also, hundreds of near-death and out-of-body experiences provide interesting insights into the period immediately after death, and these correspond very well to the hypnotic regression accounts, which can cover that period as well.

Another area where insight into death can be found is with so-called psychics, spiritualists, clairvoyants, mediums and others with the apparent ability to communicate with the spiritual realm. It is reasonable to assume that some individuals are more attuned to their spiritual natures than others, and a select few may even be able to communicate with spirits during their lives. The world is filled with people who claim to have this capability; the issue is determining which ones are for real. Although charlatans are a major concern in this area, there are some whose credentials are hard to refute, like Edgar Cayce. Well-documented accounts of much older and highly regarded psychics like Emanuel Swedenborg, who lived in the eighteenth century, are of interest as well. It is surprising how good the correlation is between psychics who lived long ago and used very different methods of obtaining spiritual knowledge and the more recent hypnotic regression patients. The following paragraphs summarize the many accounts that I found; however, I omitted many of the specifics in an effort to filter out the individual biases that might have occurred. I cannot guarantee the veracity of these accounts, but the large volume of consistent reports, on which I cannot see any reasonable way the authors could have collaborated, provides me with a confident view that there is far more truth here than opinion.

THE DEATH EXPERIENCE

Transition to Spiritual Realm

Death comes when our spirits, the conscious elements living within our bodies, permanently pull away from the senses and temporarily depart from the natural realm. It is the spirit that allows the body to maintain its form throughout life, so the body immediately begins to disintegrate when it leaves. The only part that actually dies is the physical body, as the spirit returns to the spiritual realm. Death is a material phenomenon, not a spiritual one. It is a transition from being incarnated in a physical form to existing in our natural state in the spiritual realm; nothing more, nothing less. Everyone fears death because it seems so final and unknown, but in reality death simply allows us to return to our spiritual state.

When we die we have no feelings of attachment to our corpses. They are viewed as simply chunks of material that have no importance. They are like old suits that have been discarded and no longer have any value to us. If we die when we are old or sick, we suddenly feel free, light, maneuverable, smart, young, and curious; all the things that we used to be in our youth, only to a much greater extent, but were not just before our deaths. Death is much harder on those left behind than on the person dying.

Although the process of dying can be very difficult and sometimes traumatic, death itself is usually a very pleasant experience. However, if we have an overwhelming feeling that we have sinned and deserve going to hell, we might create that experience, which won't be so pleasant. However, even the hell that we create for ourselves is eventually replaced by a more pleasant environment as we gain wisdom and understanding. As in life, in death we create our own worlds, and if we believe that we deserve hell, then our minds create it. This is a self-imposed misery an entity can escape as soon as it realizes its true nature and seriously accepts its task of perfecting itself.

Tunnel of Light

Immediately after death we see what appears to be a tunnel with a light at the end of it. This light is created by the spiritual energy of the Universal Consciousness. Although the spirit is connected to the Universal Consciousness throughout life, it is not apparent until death. Each spirit has its own unique tunnel, like an umbilical cord, that connects it to the spiritual realm. When we die we need to go through it to reach the other spirits. It is an easy transition, as all we need to do is want to go through the tunnel and it happens.

Occasionally spirits become confused and get stuck in an in-between state for a while. They may feel that they have an important task in life left undone, so they resist leaving. These spirits can appear as apparitions or ghosts to us when we are living. They rarely cause trouble and are only capable of doing so if we let them. If you ever encounter such a circumstance, just making it clear that you will not tolerate the spirit's activity will make it cease. These are confused, immature spirits that will be intimidated by a strong, forceful will. Wayward spirits can only harass us if we allow it, as we are all spirits just like them. They are generally so consumed with their past lives on earth that it takes them a while to let go; or in some unusual cases, it takes them a while to realize that they have really died. Eventually, all entities transition to the spiritual realm.

OBEs and NDEs

Our spirits permanently leave our bodies at the moment of death, but some spirits are capable of partially leaving their body for a short time while still alive, which then causes out-of-body experiences (OBEs) and near-death experiences (NDEs). This is most common in highly trau-matic situations, such as during serious medical operations or accidents. In such a case, the spirit gets confused, thinks the body is dying, and departs but eventually reenters the body, often after other spirits encourage its return. Occasionally, some people can self-induce temporary out-of-body experiences.

Greeting from Loved Ones

At the end of the tunnel we are greeted by those that we most want to see or believe that we will see. Departed friends and family are typical greeters when we first return to the spiritual realm. The main purpose of the welcoming spirits is to help us adjust to the spiritual existence. Life in the cosmos is very disorienting, and it is difficult for young spirits to readjust to a purely spiritual existence. Occasionally a mature spirit will choose to skip the introductions and go straight into his spiritual home. In most cases, the spirits are overcome by a feeling of love, which is so pleasant and strong that they do not wish to return to their bodies even if the encounter eventually becomes a near-death experience. In these cases, the individual needs to be convinced that it is in his or her best interest to return to the natural realm.

Life Review

A spiritual entity appears within a short period after death, and deeply religious people often interpret this being as Christ, Krishna, Buddha or some other deity depending on their affiliation. Nonreligious people also see this being of light but do not relate it to any specific individual. Whatever the case, the being reviews all the important events of our entire lives with us; it is like a highlight movie. The being never judges us but instead always seems especially pleased when we acted selflessly or were seeking knowledge. During our life review, *we judge ourselves,* as our conscience is our only judge! In life we are often harshly critical of others and not very critical of ourselves, but as our journey is self-directed, only we will decide how well we are doing. *No one else ever judges us*, as we are each the sole decision maker as to our progress and behavior. Many religions have errantly claimed that God judges and punishes us at death, but this is just not the case. In fact, no one ever judges someone else in the spiritual realm.

During our life reviews we experience all of the emotions that we caused others to feel. When we made someone happy we experience that person's joy. When we made someone unhappy we feel that person's sorrow and pain. The idea is not to punish or reward us for our behavior but to teach us that there is a cause-and-effect relationship for each and every one of our actions. Although there is no punishment for our misdeeds, as mistakes are expected, we must learn why these deeds are wrong and what impacts they had, both on ourselves and on others.

Reincarnation and the law of cause and effect (see below) assure that we get what we deserve and need, which are lessons to teach us the errors of our ways, not punishment for our ignorant decisions. The impacts of our mistakes, which we generate during life, only affect our own future lives and no one else's. Others may feel sorry for us if we made some bad decisions or feel happy if we made some good ones, but each of us is the only one that will have to deal with them, so our actions are of no consequence to anyone else.

In the spiritual realm, everything is open and on the table for us to see. There is no hiding behind false pretenses like here on earth. In death we come face-to-face with all of our faults and our strengths. It is our journey, and it is critical that we understand exactly where we are and where we need to go next so each experience can provide us with the greatest benefit. We are responsible for who we are and where we are, and if we do not like what we see, then only we can change it. The lessons that we still need to learn are identified in both this review and previous life reviews. We always know where we stand.

Dealing with the Death of a Loved One

We have a tendency to try to hang on to those that have recently died and are very close to us. This is counterproductive, as death is a natural process, and when someone's time on earth is over we need to let that person go and move on. Remember that there is never a circumstance in which we are left alone in the natural realm unable to cope with our problems. There is always sufficient wisdom and support for us here on earth, so we don't ever need to hold on to those that have departed. When someone that we depend on dies, it gives us an opportunity to stand on our own feet for a while. This may be disconcerting at first, but over time we will adjust to it and use it as a learning experience. Philosophy tells us that birth is really death and death is really birth. We need to accept that as truth. As hard as it may first seem, after someone close to us dies, the world moves on and we should too.

EXISTENCE IN THE SPIRITUAL REALM

In life material objects appear greater than they are and spiritual objects appear lesser. In death it is just the opposite, as we have a clearer view of reality.

Heaven and Hell

Our conception of both heaven and hell as places we go at death is unreal. Heaven and hell are states of mind, not locations. If we are truly convinced that we will go to one or the other, then that is what we will perceive at the moment of death, but this is an illusion. We create the world we live in, both in the natural realm and in the spiritual realm. The spiritual realm could be confused with heaven, but it is not the idealistic place where good people go after death to live in bliss forever, like nirvana. We have responsibilities in the spiritual realm just like we do here. Hell, on the other hand, simply does not exist outside our own minds. Hell is the torment that we put ourselves through when we consistently make selfish decisions that hurt others. We create our own hells and live in them until we are able to correct our behavior. Eventually we all begin to find truth and adjust to the realities of the spiritual realm. A better way of viewing our future is that we slowly grow into heaven through the perfection of the soul; we don't go there, heaven comes to us.

Ideas

The spiritual realm is a world of ideas. In the natural realm objects seem real and ideas appear to be fleeting and have no substance; but this could not be further from the truth. Ideas are the only things of real importance in both the natural and spiritual realms, because ideas, unlike material objects, are things that we can call our own. Even when we get an idea from another person, it immediately becomes ours as soon as we hear it. Ideas have universal ownership, as everyone gains as we become wiser. No one can or would want to take an idea away from us. We may choose to give them credit for a short period of time, but we soon absorb that idea into our core beliefs. Ideas, not objects, bring us happiness or sadness. If we are affected by an object, it is the idea of that object that affects us, not the object itself. Unlike anything else, we take ideas with us when we die because ideas belong to and reside in the spiritual realm. They are real, they are ours to do with as we wish, and they are everlasting. Ideas not only have great value, they are the only things with any value because they make us what we are. Ideas can be true or false or somewhere in between. If they are true, then they are knowledge. If they are false, then they are opinions.[30]

---

30 See chapter 7: Thought for more detail.

Realms

There are many spiritual realms, some below us in wisdom and some above. The spiritual realm that is immediately above us is the one that we exist in when we are not having life experiences. Whenever someone in this life has a mystical experience, it is in relation to entities in that particular spiritual realm. It would be very difficult for anyone to have contact with spirits in a higher realm, as it would be unlikely that he or she would be able to tune in to those vibrations. As such, the only realm that we know anything about is the next higher one. Very little information has been brought forth from the higher realms, so everything that I refer to here only applies to the next higher spiritual realm.

Appearance

When a spirit chooses to exist in the natural realm, it manifests into some specific form of its choosing, which in our case is the human body. In the spiritual realm, spirits take forms as well. Each realm has a specific type of "body" that goes with it. Because the essence of a spirit is formless, it is able to project itself into any body type it wants. So in the spiritual realm, we choose bodies compatible with that particular realm. These bodies differ from those in the natural realm in that they are of a spiritual or astral nature.

Environment

The environment that is around us in the afterlife is perceived as being very similar to that in the natural realm, only more perfect. The spiritual realm is similar to the natural realm in that it is a creation of the Universal Consciousness. There are cities with buildings and houses and roads. There are fields, lakes, and forests. It is spectacularly beautiful. There is wonderful music and art, and everything that we can imagine here on earth has a correspondent in the spiritual realm. This, of course, is the case for the next higher realm, but not necessarily for the realms beyond. The ancient adage, "As it is below, so it is above, and as it is above, so it is below"[31] holds true to an amazing extent.

There are a huge number of communities in the spiritual realm, each populated by beings that have achieved similar levels of development and are now working on related issues. It is difficult for spirits at different levels to intermingle because they all have different interests and goals. We belong to a family of spirits that work together and assist each other in accomplishing their goals while simultaneously working on their own needs. Since communities grow together, it is in everyone's best interest to assist others whenever possible. When we have accomplished everything that we need to in one community, then we move to another.

We each have a home in the afterlife that is proportionate to our wisdom. We create our homes with the help of wiser beings in a way that pleases us but stays within the boundaries of what we are allowed. The most advanced or wisest spirit in the community has the biggest and most elaborate home, but he also has the most responsibilities in regard to the functioning of the community.

As one would expect in a realm where wisdom and understanding are prized over all else, institutions of higher learning are important in the afterlife. There are dedicated places where we go for studying different aspects of our life experiences so we can better understand the effects of our decisions. Others with similar questions join us in those sessions, as do guides that can provide additional insight because they have already grasped those concepts.

Responsibilities

Everyone has responsibilities that they must address. We are not only responsible for learning new things, but also for assisting others who are coming along with or behind us. Our purpose is learning and we must continually pursue that objective.

---

31 This is part of the hermetic philosophy in the Kybalion.

LAWS

All realms are controlled by laws. These laws dictate how things work. It is impossible to ignore any spiritual law. They are like the laws of physics and must be obeyed. The Universal Consciousness can change the laws, but as long as they are active, everyone must follow them.

The Law of Cause and Effect

Cause and effect is the primary universal principle that applies in the natural realm; it teaches us right from wrong. Its premise is that all we see in this cosmos had a cause and what we see is the effect. Consequently, everything that happens from this instance forward is the effect of a past, present, or future cause. This is similar to Sir Isaac Newton's third law of physics, which states that every action has an equal but opposite reaction. The biggest difference is that Newton's law applies only to physical objects, whereas the law of cause and effect is more general and also applies to spirits. Every one of our actions will have either a positive, negative, or neutral impact on others and therefore on us. If the actions are positive or neutral then we continue along our preplanned paths that provide us additional opportunities to experience; however, if our actions have negative impacts on others, then we need to deal with those effects, which is accomplished through karma.

The Law of Karma

Controls our Experiences

The universe was created as a place where we can have learning experiences, which are controlled through a system known as karma. Karma is simply a process of cause and effect applied to the individual soul. Whenever we make a selfish decision, then karma is generated and attached to our souls. The purpose of karma is to keep track of our misunderstandings so we can eventually learn why our decisions were wrong and correct them. Karma works by allowing us to create a future circumstance that will show us another side of the issue, giving us a new perspective on the old problem. In this way we can develop a broader understanding of the issue. This is not an eye for an eye. No one is getting back at us or punishing us for our misdeeds. We are simply being shown why our previous action was a mistake. Once we understand the problem, the karma is released and the incident forgotten. For example, if we cheated someone, then we might find ourselves being cheated so we could understand how it felt. If the issue is very complex, then we may need to experience multiple circumstances to fully appreciate the nuances of the issue. Eventually we will have an opportunity to experience a situation similar to the original decision so we will have another opportunity to make a better decision. If we succeed, then the karma will be released and all will be well. If our decision is still in error, then the process continues all over again until we finally learn the lesson and make the right decision.

Correcting Misconceptions

Karma is triggered when we make someone else feel bad for our own selfish reasons. The natural state of affairs is for good things to happen to us. As such, there is no such thing as positive karma because it is not needed. There is no reward for acting well because good things automatically happen to us if we don't make mistakes. As long as we keep making wise and unselfish decisions, then good things will keep happening to us. It is only when we make selfish decisions that we need to understand our mistakes. We can view karma as a mistaken idea pushing for a correction. We look around the globe and everything seems to be in a state of chaos, but what we are really seeing are thousands of years of wars and injustices playing out through karma. The world is always in perfect balance and harmony, it is only we who are slightly out of step.

Not Punishment

Karma may seem like punishment but it really isn't. It is simply a method that leads us to the truth by showing us the error of our ways. It is like the child's game in which you tell the seeker if he is getting hotter or colder as he searches for the hidden item. Once we learn which paths lead to truth and virtue, the errors of the past are immediately forgotten. Making bad decisions is always due to ignorance, and no one is ever punished for their ignorance, but sometimes the lessons required to teach us the truth are pretty harsh. If someone is, for example, a terrorist, then he or she is not just a little bit off course; that person is so ignorant and misguided about so many things that learning all the necessary lessons takes a long time and may require many difficult lives. However, for most people the situation is not nearly as dire.

Ultimate Justice

Karma allows justice to always prevail. People are basically good, only somewhat misguided and self-centered. Caring more about others and less about ourselves will have an immediate positive impact on our lives. Karma teaches through the principle of experiencing opposite sides of a situation. If we commit a murder, then we might experience being murdered. The more unselfish service we do for others, the more we will experience unselfish acts done for us. Karma assures justice for all.

Makes Us Unique

Karma goes hand in hand with reincarnation and guarantees that every life is unique. Although we all learn the same truths, our different lessons give us different perspectives on them. Every experience that we have is in some minor way different from any experience that someone else has ever had, which makes us all different in our own right. We each react differently to a common set of experiences than anyone ever did or ever will. In our lives, we set forth unique sets of causes that result in unique effects, and the universe is then changed uniquely by each of us. The general lessons are not unique, as they apply to every spiritual being. It is the circumstances surrounding each lesson and the being that is learning it that are unique. This is what keeps life interesting throughout eternity; everything is always different and always changing.

Makes Us Responsible

The laws of reincarnation, karma, and cause and effect make us each responsible for our own decisions. Each of us has free will to do as we please, and each of us is on an individual journey. We are the only ones responsible for our own progress; no one else suffers for our indiscretions. When we injure someone in life, that person learns a lesson that he or she undoubtedly needed, and we suffer the consequence by generating karma that we will eventually be forced to resolve. Our sense of personal responsibility increases as we grow, so the more advanced we become, the more we expect from ourselves.

PREPARATION FOR THE NEXT LIFE

Death should be viewed as a positive experience because it is an opportunity for us to break our negative patterns of behavior and reorient our lives. As young souls, it is easy to get in selfish patterns of materialism and greed. Death gets us out of these karma-generating situations that we get stuck in and allows us to regroup, understand the mistakes that we have made, and start fresh. Eventually we begin to make better choices. Death provides us with opportunities for corrective actions before we let ourselves get too far astray.

The Return to Life

No one rushes us back into a life before he or she is ready. We do not have to reincarnate immediately, but eventually we will want to because we all aspire to perfect our souls. If we have had a difficult life, we can take our time before we come back. We can rest and digest our life and indeed we can set up an easier life in order to get ourselves back on track. We need to eventually work off all our karma, but we don't want to put ourselves in situations where we are likely to make the wrong decisions that will increase our karma. We only return to the natural realm when we are ready.

In death our primary purpose is to digest our past lives. Advanced souls take longer to assimilate their experiences than younger ones because their lives are more complicated. A very advanced soul may take several thousand years before reincarnating again, whereas someone that died very young will reincarnate very quickly. Less than one hundred years might be typical for most souls on earth. Plato believed the material world had a gravitational draw on our souls, but as our spirits become more advanced the returning force becomes less and less until the soul escapes from the force of the natural realm altogether. But until that happens, we are continually drawn back into the sphere of unfinished business until all of our issues are resolved.

The Life Plan

Prioritizing Lessons

When our past lives are fully digested, we are able to begin crafting our new plan for the next life, which is our life plan. At death, we begin evaluating what we accomplished in previous lives, especially the last one, and prioritizing what we still need to work on. It is difficult to assimilate a complicated and full life. We need to study and understand what went well and why and what needs to be changed. Every truth needs to be learned eventually, but because this is a building process, certain truths have more value to us than others, so we will want to learn them first. It's like needing to learn to read before studying English literature. We establish our goals and decide which lessons are the most important for us at this point in our journey and then set out a plan to accomplish those goals.

Guides or Masters

We have very wise guides that act as our advisors when we are selecting the lessons to learn and the experiences that will best teach us those lessons. This is usually a trio of entities that have far surpassed our level of wisdom. Although we can work on anything that we choose, our guides always know best. If our guides recommend a difficult life to teach us about a serious issue, we can choose to ignore their wise counsel, but inevitably it will be at our peril. Since our journey is self-directed and we have free will, if we choose a path that goes against our guides' recommendations, then we are allowed to take it. We will surely learn certain lessons, but they may not be the ones that we expected; and generally those spirits that do not follow their guides' recommendations will have difficult lives and create even more karma.

Creating the Body

Our spirits, with help from our spirit guides, create our bodies using the boundaries of the human species template along with our parents' DNA. Each species has an archetypal template that was created in the spiritual realm and establishes the limits within which a body can exist and take form. However, each spirit has considerable flexibility as to appearance, health, aptitude, and other such characteristics. A spirit usually first engages the embryo at conception in order to assist in its growth, because the spirit has a specific set of goals that it wants to accomplish during each incarnation. The spirit influences the body not only during embryonic growth, but also throughout childhood, adolescence, and adulthood in order to assist it in providing an advantageous body/environment, which will allow it to best achieve its goals. Our bodies are reflections of our mental energy, and their shapes reflect the nature of our souls. Of course, each person's attitude, motivation, character, will, desires, and emotions are all unique. This is why siblings and even identical twins that grow up in the same household are very different personalities. However, when people choose to be twins, they probably have similar goals to accomplish, so one might expect that even if separated at birth, they could have created somewhat similar lives.

Props

We mutually choose our parents, children, extended family, and friends we want to work with during each life. We could be a poor Indian girl in one life and a wealthy Irishman in the next. It all depends on what circumstance we want to experience during life and what lesson we want to learn next. Every life is equal, no matter what the material circumstances are surrounding it.

The life plan is remembered in the subconscious. As such, during life the subconscious creates an environment that is conducive to meeting our goals. This includes causing us to make day-to-day decisions that create experiences with the necessary circumstances required to learn each lesson. For example, the subconscious will go so far as to cause an accident that disables us if we want to experience disability midway through a life. Because the universe is like a stage, each of us creates the props that we need to act out our dramas, which include physical and mental handicaps, along with special capabilities.

Impact of our Decisions

When we learn a lesson we can go on to another lesson, but if we don't adequately deal with the initial lesson, then a situation will appear in which we get a second or third opportunity to learn the lesson. There is no getting away from the plan. The sooner we deal with our problems, the sooner we can get on to other things. We have the free will to make each and every decision as we choose, but our subconscious minds are predisposed to act in a way that will give us the experiences we need.

Those of us that appear to be inclined toward selfish acts will face many difficult lives before learning the error of our ways, so the sooner that we learn these lessons, the sooner we can get ourselves back on more enjoyable tracks. In fact, some spirits get so far off course that they don't want to have life experiences at all because they do not want to face the difficulties in the natural realm. But eventually we all must return and continue the struggle toward perfection. The sooner we develop a positive attitude about life and embrace our difficulties, the sooner we can begin to enjoy the process.

Gradually we take on more responsibility for the creation of our life plans. Initially our guides need to direct our experiences, but as we become wiser, we are better able to make many of those decisions. This includes creating more selfless lives and helping others have successful life experiences. We need to help create a world that we and others want to live in.

Guardian Angels

In addition to the three very wise guides who are fully cognizant of every aspect of our beings, we have one or more spirit guides, often referred to as guardian angels, that watch out for us throughout our lifetimes to ensure nothing unexpected happens and we are able to execute our life plans. They are always with us and will communicate with and assist us whenever necessary. In fact, when we experience near-miss accidents and think how lucky we were, it probably was not luck at all. It was most likely our spirit guides interceding on our behalf so that some unplanned event did not occur. Everything that happens has a higher purpose than what is readily apparent. The spirit guides know what we will most likely do in every circumstance and are prepared for our decisions well in advance of any event. They are fully aware of what we are supposed to accomplish and provide any needed assistance, whether we ask for it or not. There are very few real accidents in this world. Also, when we think that we are talking to God or some other religious figure, it is most likely our spirit guides; we are never alone.

Forgetting

When we incarnate, we lose access to our spiritual memories but we don't forget our spiritual wisdom. Each life is suppose to start with a blank slate as far as past experiences are concerned, but who we are and our fundamental beliefs are still part of us. Our conscious minds cannot easily tap into our huge wealth of knowledge, however, what we call instinct and subconscious is really a fuzzy and somewhat opaque window into our forgotten past. Past-life experiences are purposely hidden, but sometimes this doesn't happen quite as completely as normal. When a spirit feels that it has left something very important undone in its past life, it may return before it has had time to fully digest its life experiences. If it returns very quickly, it may have unusually strong past-life memories. This can result in children remembering previous lives or child geniuses. When a three-year-old like Mozart can write symphonies, it is because he has strong past-life memories. It is possible for some people with more psychic abilities to get clearer glimpses of this information than others, but even the most capable seers only have superficial access to their spiritual knowledge.

ASTROLOGY

Astrology has a bad name in many circles because it is misapplied by its practitioners and as a result misunderstood by the general public. Astrology was a science to the ancients because they understood the physics of the phenomena. The understanding of what astrology really is and how it works has been lost over time, so now we are simply applying the rules as best we can and in hopes nothing has changed.

Through the years, the Eastern practitioners seem to have been able to retain a more accurate methodology than Westerners.

The basic concept of astrology is fairly straightforward, although science has not yet re-created the physics to explain it. The concept is that every celestial body, be it a planet, sun, moon, asteroid, star, or star group, has an energy vibration or pattern emanating from it, as does every other object in the cosmos, no matter how small it is. These planetary vibrations put an imprint on a newborn body that predisposes it to certain personality traits. A body is most susceptible to these traits when it is first born (possibly because it is no longer shielded by the mother's ethereal, astral, and mental fields). The position of each heavenly body in relation to the child's specific location on earth at its birth determines the influence each celestial object has on the child. As part of the selection of our parents, we select our places and dates of birth in order to assist in predisposing us to learn certain lessons. As such, we are assisted in the execution of our life plans by where and when we are born. For example, if we want to learn the lessons that are best learned as a musician, having a body that is more musically inclined would be an advantage.

Astrologers believe they can predict what the solar system's personality bias is. They also believe certain heavenly combinations are better for some dispositions than others, which is the basis of our daily horoscopes. This is a very old science, and many people argue that astrology today has lost its ability to accurately predict our natures. Jeffrey Armstrong[32] claims that Western astrology is using calculations that are twenty-three degrees different than actual star locations, which causes huge errors. However, I would be somewhat cautious in reading too much significance into anybody's daily horoscope until physics turns it back into a science.

Remember that astrology is strictly a low-grade bias on our personalities. It is not a strong determining force. Our free will always overrules any of these influences.

---

32 Jeffrey Armstrong, *God The Astrologer*, page 33.

CREATING OUR WORLDS

Our spirituality[33] is the life we each lead; our mentality or ego is the builder of that life; and our body is the result. Each time the ego builds a body, it builds a better one.

The world that we live in is a mirror image of our thoughts. Our jobs, homes, families, lifestyles, etc., reflect our inner convictions and desires. It is a creation that we built over our lifetimes. It appears that we are all living together in the same world, but in reality, we are each in our own little self-created world, which we have fine-tuned for our personal needs. The worlds that we create are as unique as we are, because each of us is trying to accomplish different things with different agendas, while at the same time working together to help others live their lives. Even our mates are experiencing very different lives than we are. Our desires, goals, hopes, and expectations were the building blocks that we used for life's foundation. We each see and experience the world uniquely because our worlds are our creations.

We can only really know ourselves. Two people can attend the same event, and one can view it very positively and have a rewarding experience, while the other can see it as negative; the same event with two perspectives. This is because our experiences all take place in our minds. As such, it is only our perceptions of the event that matter, not the event itself. Our experience is totally dependent on how we react to the circumstance, not the circumstance itself. Our highly crafted cosmos consists of billions of individual lives, all intermeshing together. Our lives are shared with others, but our past experiences and biases slant our views in a special way. Sometimes we may think of ourselves as spectators, but we are really always participants. If we attend a football game, we might be spectators of the game, but we are participants of the event. No matter how close we are to another person, even a soul mate,

33 See chapter 8: Spirituality.

we can never truly understand what others are thinking and how they feel, as the only one we can know and understand is our self.

Above all else, we should enjoy the journey, both in life and in the afterlife. We need to appreciate the problems that we set up for ourselves, laugh at the magnitude of the messes we have created, but stay positive at all times! Life and the people with whom we associate are meant to be enjoyed. We don't need to be unhappy learning our lessons. In fact, quite the opposite, we are supposed to enjoy the journey; but then again, that is our choice as well.

CHAPTER 5

SELFLESS SERVICE

Know, O man, ye should aim at perfection,
for only thus can ye attain to the goal.
Though ye should know that nothing is perfect,
yet it should be thy aim and thy goal.

— The Emerald Tablets

Key Concept:	Selfishness is the cause of all mankind's troubles.

SELFISHNESS

The focus of the life plan is to work off the karma we generated in past lives and avoid creating any more karma in this lifetime. As such, it is important to understand how karma is generated and then act accordingly.

The ideological founders of two of the most influential and disparate religions in man's history, Buddha and Jesus, agreed on a single primary principle they believed was holding man back from nirvana or eternal life: selfishness. Buddha said that living a selfless life was the only way that man could be released from this world's suffering. Jesus said that man needed to love God and his neighbor as much as he loved himself. It also appears that the ancient civilization had a similar perspective. We have all heard the words but have not heeded the message. The most important truth in life is the error of selfishness, as it is the source of all karma.

THE GOLD STANDARD

The Universal Consciousness's requirement to perfect the soul is simply stated and well-known to all:

Always put others above ourselves.

Or, stated in the negative:

Eliminate all selfish behavior.

If everyone followed this wisdom, then crime, greed, war, poverty, and most of our legal and governmental systems would soon disappear; but this is far easier said than done.

ASPECTS OF SELFISHNESS

Selfishness is so deep-rooted within us that if we are going to change our ways we need to recognize the magnitude of the problem so we can begin to deal with it.

Extreme Selfishness

Crime is by far the most extreme form of selfish behavior. Allowing ourselves to be so egotistical that we force our will on others generates a huge karmic response and this karma is not easily overcome. Physical crimes like murder, arson, theft etc. are obvious acts of selfishness. Terrorism is the epitome of criminal activity as there is nothing more selfish than indiscriminately killing or maiming others and the resulting karma will cause many difficult lives. However, violent crime is not the only act with serious karmic consequences. Sophisticated white collar crimes are egotistical actions that cause hardship and pain for many people and the lessons here can be very difficult as well. These crimes are obvious and the penalties are great but most of us do not participate in this type of extreme activity.

The Working World

There are many instances that occur especially in our business life where we make decisions that we feel are good for us without considering the full impact on others. For example is it right to charge as much as the rich are willing to pay for a life saving drug or even just a pain reducer if we know that it causes hardship for many and excludes some? Is it right for the legal community to make doctors pay for honest mistakes of judgment and in the process run up the cost of health care for everyone? Is it right to accept unemployment compensation when we could go back to work but prefer not to? Is it right for executives to receive large compensations when they have not correspondingly improved the welfare of their companies? Is it right to let a dictator slaughter his people if we have a means to stop it? Every industry, every job, every person is faced with difficult and subtle issues of right and wrong every day. There are no yes and no answers to any of these questions because the circumstances surrounding them can be so varied. Even the simplest question of 'is theft immoral' could have special circumstances for a life saving situation. We often look at a situation and convince ourselves that what we are doing is legal but we seldom take the next step and ask ourselves if it is right. All too often we simply do what we think is best for us.

Everyday Life

Most of us would say we live honest lives, give to charities, and support people that are down and out. We belong to religious and community organizations that help people in need and always contribute to the good causes that continually arise at the office. This is all well and good and confirms that we are kind souls at heart, but remember that our goal is reaching a state of wisdom that allows us to escape the cosmic cycle of life and death. Clearly we have not reached it yet, or I would not be writing this book and you would not be reading it. The pursuit of perfection requires that we raise our level of conduct to a higher standard. To do this we need to look at our lives and see where our behavior might be letting us down. Selfishness is exhibited in very subtle ways and so ingrained within our nature we rarely give it a second thought. There are many seemingly harmless selfish acts that we do every day that over time add up to a pretty selfish perspective:

1. Accepting the wrong change at the store when it is in our favor

2. Pushing ahead of others in line

3. Accepting unemployment benefits when we could actually get a job

4. Fudging on our taxes

5. Misrepresenting our experience on our résumés

6. Spreading false rumors in the office

7. Accepting undue accolades

8. Using an inaccurate golf handicap

9. Driving recklessly

10. Showing off or making others feel bad

11. Goofing off at work

12. Losing our tempers

13. Ignoring someone that needs assistance

14. Being rude

15. Needing the nicest house and car

This list could go on and on, but the point is that we all do selfish things in our lives without even thinking about them; selfishness is second nature to us. The need for material success and praise overwhelms us as we compare ourselves to others along the way. Too many welfare recipients pride themselves on how much they can get out of the system not how fast they can get back into the workforce. Too many union leaders care more about what they can get out of the company than how they can contribute to its betterment. Too many executives care more about their compensation packages than their customers' satisfaction. Too many politicians care more about staying in power than the welfare of the country or the world. Even large charity donors want their names on everything their money builds. It goes on and on. We look for a way to beat the system because we want to be the best or the first or the most noticed. Instead of focusing our efforts on improving ourselves, we focus on outdoing others. In sports we hold Green Bay's legendary coach, Vince Lombardi, up as the ideal. His motto, "Winning isn't everything, it is the only thing," is hardly a standard to live by. If we want to perfect our souls, we need to change "winning" to "selfless service."

To perfect our souls, we need to realize that what we are doing is wrong and why. We view our selfish behavior as acceptable because everyone else does it, but then everyone else is also stuck here with us in this cycle of life and death.

Ethics

If we want to improve ourselves, one of the first steps is to look at our ethics. The planet is full of good people that have lost their way because they lack strong moral compasses to guide them when choices become conflicting and confusing. Governments across the globe employ a multitude of regulatory agencies with literally millions of people who are creating and enforcing laws to prevent people from acting in selfish ways. Not only is this a colossal waste of time and money, but it is a hopeless task, since for every law they create there are an equal number of people figuring ways to circumvent that law. In fact, many countries have given in to selfishness in the form of graft to such an extant it has become a way of life. When we focus on winning the battle for material gains, we end up losing the spiritual war. If we had a better set of ethics we would be better prepared to deal with the complicated world in which we find ourselves.

Often our ethics are ill defined and take a back seat to materialistic self-interests. Most people try to act ethically most of the time, at least for the big decisions, but it is difficult to make the right decision when so many people are continually acting selfishly toward us and we feel we must compete to attain material rewards. People do not go into politics with the express interest of making money, yet all too many of our politicians use their offices for personal gain. People do not go into business intending to stab a fellow worker in the back, but on their way up the ladder they find themselves doing it. We don't start our careers expecting to take advantage of others, but the pressures we put on ourselves to succeed and the lack of a solid moral code let us get off track. Everywhere we look we find people that have started out with good intentions but have gotten swept up by the system.

ETHICS AND VIRTUE

Detachment

Many mystics teach that living a life of detachment is the key to breaking the cycle of rebirth. In this case detachment means we are not emotionally tied to the material rewards of our tasks. If rewards come to us then so be it; but it is our experiences and the knowledge gained from them that are what is important, not the recognition or compensation that we receive. In fact, if our motivation is the material reward, our selfishness will detract from those lessons. However, detachment does not mean that we should not care about the results of our efforts or the quality of our work; in fact, quite the opposite. We are supposed to do our very best at whatever we choose to do. Detachment simply means that we are unaffected by the rewards that are attached to the effort. The only true reward is the lesson that we learn. Everything else will rapidly fade into the past.

Standards of Conduct

A truly virtuous deed brings no remorse and only happiness. Virtuous, ethical, and selfless behaviors must be the same thing, as all three demand excellent conduct. If our ethics do not define a standard of excellent behavior, then we will not be heading toward our goal of perfection. In order to improve our behavior, we need to study the issues, evaluate situations, and become more aware of the effects of our actions. If we want to follow our life plans, our behavior must be virtuous. All codes of ethics need to be based on putting others above ourselves.

An unselfish person is as pleased when a coworker gets the promotion as he is when he gets it. Virtuous people want others to have as many material possessions as they have, earn as much money as they do, and live lives as healthy and happy as they do. In other words, a truly selfless person wants all others to have every benefit he or she has. This is a very difficult standard to live by, but it is a necessary goal if we are to break the karmic bonds that tie us to this world. Few people on earth have reached this standard of conduct.

The only way to have a virtuous society is for us all to understand that it is in our best interests. We establish laws that penalize criminals, but even they only address the most extreme aspects of our behavior.

Laws make activities illegal, but they hardly protect us; our only real protection is that most people are good enough not to live selfish lives of crime. The path of virtue needs to be chosen, not mandated or threatened, and it needs to be part of our psyches.

EDUCATION

Code of Ethics

Socrates and Protagoras wrestled with the concept of whether virtue could be taught, and at one time or another they both seemingly defended each side of the argument; in the end, neither came to a conclusion. I suspect that was because virtuous actions require two things: (1) the desire to live virtuously, and (2) the knowledge of what constitutes virtue. The former may or may not be taught by man, but surely the latter can and must be taught. Although virtue cannot be regulated or forced upon us, we need to at least understand what it means. At a minimum, we need to decide what virtue is so that those who choose to lead a finer existence can at least understand what their choices are.

We have watered down our view of ethical behavior from the days of Socrates to such an extent that we don't even view it as the same thing as virtuous behavior. To live lives of integrity, we need to live by an ethical code that is virtuous. We need to raise our standards.

A code of ethics will need to be created that will assist us every step along the way. We are not bad people; we just have bad habits, and bad habits require effort to overcome. Our education system needs to address these issues. Education cannot make us virtuous, but it can make us aware of our choices. Eventually we will all decide to follow the path of goodness as we realize the error of any other existence. Living the gold standard is a vision of the future, not a practical expectation for most of us today. What we need is an ethical path that will lead us from where we are today to that standard. We should begin by teaching this code at the very earliest period in our children's growth when they can first perceive right and wrong.

Primary and Secondary Education

The goal of education must be changed to teach us to become morally superior people, as goodness and wisdom go hand in hand. We need to instill in our children a higher sense of purpose than materialism. They need to appreciate that effort is its own reward and seeking recognition for their efforts is counterproductive.

Ethics as a curriculum needs to be a key aspect of all education, from nursery school up through high school. We teach our children the fundamentals of ethics, but they get the subtleties by osmosis. They watch us as parents, teachers, and role models living selfish lives, and it is easy to see why children learn to be out for themselves. Then we let them spend hours watching TV, where virtue is as rare as hen's teeth. Leaving this critical piece of their education up to chance is unacceptable. Our society needs to be focused on ethics until it becomes second nature.

As part of this effort to insert virtue into our education system, we need to stop whitewashing our curricula and stress the importance of truth in every aspect of our teaching. Our history books, for example, present a totally distorted view of reality. Mankind's history, including politics, religion, and wars, has been one selfish endeavor after another. As we look back into past civilizations, we should recognize the shortcomings of those who went before us, not to judge them, but to learn from their mistakes, because in reality those who went before were really us. We can ill afford to make the same mistakes again. We also must stress the true positives that have made our country so great. Teaching our history from a perspective of cultural achievement rather than wars and conquests would be a good start.

Another key element of an ethical education would be to teach new generations how to find and follow their life plans. If our purpose in this life is to have certain experiences, some of which will be difficult, then we should understand that at a very early age and begin to prepare for it. We need to teach children who they are, why they are here, and what they need to do to reduce the karma they have already accumulated. Children need to learn to embrace their difficulties and appreciate those around them who enabled those experiences, no matter what role they played. How we deal with life determines how well we will succeed in executing our life plans.

Our educational system needs to stress personal responsibility. We need to appreciate that we are responsible for the consequences of our actions, whether they are obvious or extenuating. The impact of our efforts is more far-reaching than we recognize. When we make decisions, either selfish or virtuous, they cause much greater effects than we perceive. We need to realize that we are responsible for those effects and the karma they might generate.

Higher Education

Ethics at the collegiate and professional education levels needs as much emphasis as at the elementary and secondary levels because the issues in the working world are so sophisticated. It is here where the ethical issues really become opaque. Our present higher education system virtually ignores ethics. We teach the basics of finance, engineering, politics, law, etc., but totally disregard the subtleties of their applications and the impact of the daily decisions made in real life. The worlds of business, government, and education all bring their own unique issues to the table, and we need to understand how to deal with them. Each subject area needs to accept the responsibility of establishing a specialized moral code that addresses the issues where its particular discipline impacts society. Our universities and trade schools are woefully negligent in establishing guidelines and teaching the sophisticated aspects of ethics. If we want people to act ethically, we must at least help them decide what that is.

A LIFE OF VIRTUE

The ultimate task of perfecting the soul is living a life of virtue.

If we want to improve our lives, we need to put the same effort into our ethical behavior as we have put into chasing material wealth. Our society has put a great deal of time, money, and effort into science and technology because those increased our physical comforts and offered diverse entertainment, but along with the creature comforts came a distorted view of truth and a debilitating level of stress and frustration. Our material accomplishments provide momentary pleasure, but they cannot maintain that feeling for long, as contentment is not derived from physical objects.

Changing our ethical standards requires changing our value system. How we treat each other is the single most important aspect of our lives. We need to strive to put others ahead of ourselves at all times. This demands a huge change of attitude, and it will take a good bit of time to adjust our priorities. We don't need to get it all right immediately, but if we can at least recognize where we need to go, we will be able to ease this most difficult part of our journey.

Prejudice needs to be addressed in every nook and cranny of our society. It is no accident that our bodies are created to look and act differently. The races, cultures, and mores that make us appear to be different give us the opportunity to experience the feelings of intolerance, prejudice, superiority, inferiority, etc. This is useful up to a point, because we cannot understand sympathy and tolerance until we feel the negative effects of prejudice; but as a world society, prejudice has gotten out of hand, and we need to bring it back in line. Introspection is needed to understand why we feel the way we do about people who appear and act differently than we do. It is only the outward appearance that fools us into perceiving differences as we are all the same. Virtue is accepting others for what they are, not what they look like.

We and only we are responsible for our thoughts and actions. Above all else, we must never fool ourselves! When we follow a doctrine that we don't really understand just to make our lives more comfortable, we are only deceiving ourselves and running away from the issues with which we need to deal. Deceiving others has its own set of problems, but deceiving ourselves makes it impossible to follow our life plans. Once we get off course, it is very hard to get back to where we need to be. Who we are and where we are has been determined by the decisions we alone have made. Who we become and how we get there will be determined by our decisions not yet made. Virtue is not just treating others well, but also treating ourselves well. Virtue today is of paramount importance for happiness tomorrow!

Hermes[34] believed that the appreciation for universal good is the beginning of wisdom. We are the sum total of our thoughts, and *"no man can know more than he himself is"*[35]; if we want to know more, then we need to become more by creating for ourselves virtuous natures.

JUSTICE

We need to be cautious that we do not confuse a code of ethics with a legal system. Strictly speaking, ethics incorporates all manner of how we act, including laws, but laws are a special form of ethics because they only address the most egregious activities, in which people are considered dangers to society. Ethics is generally viewed as a set of codes of behavior that extends up to the legal system but does not include it. Ethics covers how we think we should treat each other and is a measure of our

---

34 Hermes Trismegistus is thought to be the Egyptian god Thoth and the Greek god Hermes. He is reputed to have been the source of the hermetic philosophy.

35 Manly P. Hall, *Words to the Wise*, page 41.

integrity; laws cover how we must treat each other and are a measure of our honesty. Both legal and ethical systems need to be just and virtuous. Man encourages people to live honestly through the court systems; God ensures we learn to live virtuously through the law of karma. Theocracies, where religion and government are intertwined, have a tendency to confuse these roles as they try to extend man's laws to cover ethical situations in the name of God, which inevitably results in tyranny. As the saying goes, *"Wise men speak of God, but foolish men speak for God."*[36]

A good way to check our views is to ask ourselves: "If my thoughts were laws, would there be justice in my world?" We live in a world where all too often we impose our beliefs on others in the name of morality, but morality comes from within. We have no right to save people from themselves by forcing our ethics on them, because our ethics may not be right no matter how pure we view ourselves. We are all learning and changing, and who is to say that what we believe now is truth? We exist in a state of transition. Advising and assisting others is fine, but there is a fine line between helping others and imposing our wills on them. There is nothing moral about telling other people what to do when they are only affecting themselves. Societies consist of subcultures in the form of religions, political parties, and other social organizations, and each has its own view of what is acceptable and unacceptable. People should be free to do as they please as long as they are not inflicting their lifestyles and views on others. Prohibition is a good example of where the self-righteousness of the few inflicted hardship on the many. If an activity is truly victimless and the only person impacted is the perpetrator, then there should be no criminal or moral offense. There is no justice in making others live the way we think is best, as morality needs to be chosen, not regulated. The law of karma will eventually show everyone the true path, so it behooves us to worry more about ourselves and leave others alone.

---

36 Manly P. Hall, *Words to the Wise*, page 126.

KEY TO CONTENTMENT

When we follow our life plans, we feel a sense of accomplishment and inner peace. When we don't we are restless, disturbed, and if we are far enough off course, we feel despair or even hatred. Although our actions may appear to be aimed at others, in reality our real feelings and frustrations are aimed at ourselves. Nobody's spiritual plan is the pursuit of wealth or fame for its own end. If either comes as a result of natural endeavors, so be it, but if that is our focus in life, then our selfish desires have taken over our spiritual natures. A society in which people focus primarily on their own egotistical desires makes life difficult for everyone.

Selfless service to others is the sure path to contentment and higher cycles of existence.

CHAPTER 6

ILLUSIONS

Know, O man, that Light is thine heritage.
Know that darkness is only a veil.
Sealed in thine heart is brightness eternal,
waiting the moment of freedom to conquer,
waiting to rend the veil of the night.

Given to man have they secrets
that shall guard and protect him from all harm.
He who would travel the path of the master,
free must he be from the bondage of night.
Conquer must he the formless and shapeless,
conquer must he the phantom of fear.

– The Emerald Tablets

Key Concept: **The purpose of the cosmos is to allow spirits**
to learn about themselves and seek wisdom.

THE SEARCH FOR WISDOM

Inside each of us is a desire to find truth. It began as only a spark, but as we progress along our journey, it burns brighter and brighter until at last it becomes an all-consuming flame. The spark was lit when our seedling spirit was released into the cosmos and has been nurtured at every turn by the Universal Consciousness. Ignorance is misery and wisdom is the only way out.

Medieval knights searched the world for the Holy Grail in hopes of obtaining everlasting life, but the long-sought chalice that supposedly offered mankind eternal life was not a cup after all; it was truth consumed at the altar of knowledge and wisdom. Alchemists[37] likened the soul of mankind to lead and the illuminated soul to gold. Alchemy is the work that needs to be done to illuminate mankind, and the philosophers' stone is the wisdom that transforms man's soul into its divine entity.

The Universal Consciousness chose the cosmos to be the vehicle to teach us truth. The chosen method was to fabricate illusions that would create learning experiences. It was necessary for the illusion to seem real enough to fully engage our emotions in order for us to completely understand all aspects of truth as they relate to our emotions. Here is how it works.

THE ILLUSION

Cosmos

The cosmos is not as it appears to be, as we live in a world of illusion. Plato explained it well in *The Republic* when he said (I paraphrase): *life is as if we are sitting in a cave with our backs to the light. As we gaze upon the shadows on the wall, which is all we can see, we search for truth. But the real truth is the light source behind us that we don't see. We simply see the illusions on the cave walls.* The Universal

---

37 Alchemy is a medieval term that originated in the secret societies of Europe and was explained publicly as the chemistry of turning common metals like lead into precious metals like gold. However, within the secret societies it had a covert meaning, in that it described the process of the soul's evolution from the crude and ignorant state of mankind into the wise and refined state of a god.

Consciousness is not only the light that Plato was referring to, but it is also the shadows on the wall. Everything that exists is part of the Universal Consciousness; it is the All. It is all we can see and all that is behind us.

The illusion of the cosmos is mistakenly perceived in several ways. (1) The cosmos is not the stand-alone, self-created, and permanent entity that it appears to be. It is the temporary creation of the spiritual realm. (2) Every object created by nature is alive and has a controlling spirit residing within it. The Universal Consciousness consists of an infinite number of conscious units, and some of those units are embedded within the natural realm and are hidden from man by their many disguises. The universe is composed of energy in the form of matter that is shaped into an untold multitude of objects. Although every object has a spiritual being attached to it and is controlled by it, these beings cannot be perceived by our five senses. Each material form is able to grow, live, and die because of the actions of the controlling embodied spirit. For example, a forest has one or more spirits that are attached to it and control all its life cycle activities. Although each individual tree may not have its own dedicated spirit, every tree has a spirit that controls its growth. When the spirit departs, the object dies. This is true of all material things that are found in nature, including flora and fauna, rocks, planets, stars, and even galaxies. Everything in the cosmos has a controlling spirit. The appearance and self-sufficiency of the natural realm is simply an illusion. (3) The multitude of objects, which we think of as nature, do not permanently reside in this universe. They only reside here temporarily in order to experience life conditions. The cosmos is real and truly exists, but it is an illusion because it is not what it appears to be.

Our Senses Create the Illusion

Although we always remain in the spiritual realm, our minds are so overloaded with the illusions of life that we fail to see the true spiritual reality from which the cosmos emanates. In other words we are living in an altered state of reality. We don't see the transcendent spiritual realm that has created and continues to maintain the natural realm because the natural realm enfolds our spirits within it. Truth, which is the spiritual realm embedded in the natural realm, is obscured by our five senses. Our senses perceive energy vibrations and turn them into a consistent picture that we see, hear, feel, smell, and taste and then interpret as our world. This illusion is for our benefit because it allows us to immerse ourselves in this world and in so doing take ownership of our experiences.

Nature of the Cosmos

The Illusion of the cosmos is nothing more than an endless stream of thought created and maintained by the Universal Consciousness. *This is a difficult but important aspect of reality to grasp.* In our minds, thoughts come and go continuously in an endless string with no apparent discontinuities. We jump from one thought to another, but we never stop thinking. If each of our thoughts were a picture, our thought pattern would look like a movie scene, constantly changing but never stopping. Because our minds are not well disciplined, the scenes would skip from one subject to another, but they would never cease happening. The universe is no different, except that it is maintained by a great deal more capable and disciplined mind, so there are no apparent discontinuities.

Let me make it totally clear: the illusion really exists, just like Plato's shadows on the cave wall really existed. It is only an illusion because we cannot see what causes it and we do not realize that it is a temporary creation of a mind. The concept of the illusion is really hard to grasp because it goes against what we perceive in day-to-day life, but it is no stranger than what quantum mechanics tells us is reality. In fact, it is consistent with David Bohm's[38] concept of quantum mechanics described in his book *Wholeness and The Implicate Order*.

It is because a mind has created the cosmos that thought can control matter[39]. The fact that our minds are part of the Universal Consciousness is what allows us to be able to influence our world and the matter within it. Our minds can only influence a very small portion of the natural realm because we are only very small portions of the Universal Consciousness. The universe is a thought, admittedly a very complicated and detailed thought, but a thought just the same.

The illusion makes it appear that the material world is the only reality, and we are an integral part of it. This illusion is enhanced by the fact that when our spirits incarnate we are so entwined with our physical bodies that we cannot distinguish between the two. For millennia philosophers have been asking the questions: When we see, who sees? When we think, who thinks? When we feel, who feels? Mainstream science tells us it is the brain that sees, thinks, and feels, but in fact it is the spirit that transcends the body.

ASPECTS OF THE ILLUSION

Frequency and Time Domains

The spiritual realm is eternal and time has no meaning within it. A spirit is composed of energy consisting of different frequencies and amplitudes, so it is better understood in the frequency domain as opposed to the time domain with which we are so familiar. Each spirit exists in a certain vibratory or frequency state, which can be described by the

---

38 David Bohm studied relativity with Einstein but separated from him over a disagreement on quantum mechanics. Bohm wrote *Quantum Theory* in 1951, which might be the best book ever written explaining the subject. In 1980 Bohm wrote *Wholeness and The Implicate Order*, explaining how the oddities of the universe described by quantum mechanics might work. In it he proposed how there must be an implied order behind the universe of which we are unaware.

39 See chapter 7: Thought for more detail.

frequency characteristics of its composite energies. In an eternal spiritual world, everything exists in the now. In the spiritual world, when we look back to our previous, less wise condition, we look back to previous mental states that we were in, not to previous times or locations.

Unlike the spiritual realm, the natural realm is better understood by viewing it in the time domain. Science tells us time only exists in our space-time continuum, which is our universe. Time is the fourth dimensional axis that is attached to our three spatial dimensions. Inherently we recognize that everything in our lives is constantly changing from day to day, hour to hour, and even moment to moment. Nothing stays the same because the entire cosmos is continuously in motion relative to itself. When the cosmos ceases to exist, then time does as well. Time has no meaning when it is not tied to space. Time and space are part of the illusion because they only exist in the natural realm.

Another way to look at it is that a spirit changes state as it grows; it does not change locations. It may change locations within the cosmos for other purposes, but it is not as a result of its intellectual growth. However, in the natural realm, a change of location is often synonymous with growth. We change classrooms as we progress in school, we change schools, houses, jobs, offices, etc., when we advance throughout our lives. We may also change intellectually, but we don't notice that aspect of ourselves. This is all part of the illusion. We know we are evolving, but we do not see it as changes of state as much as position changes. Neither perspective is either right or wrong; they are just the way we view life.

Change

The nature of the material cosmos is dynamic, energetic, beautiful, and constantly in motion. Nothing ever stays the same. The ever-changing cosmos allows us to have a constant stream of new experiences. The cosmos is like a river that cleanses itself by washing away the pollution of the past. Ideas in the cosmos are the water droplets in the river, and the pollutants are the false opinions that we cling to.

Changes are always for the good, but we see such a small slice of reality at any one time that we don't understand the full implication of a change when it first occurs. However, when we view our existences over many lifetimes, we will realize each new circumstance provided us with a new opportunity to experience some aspect of truth. We need to embrace change no matter how difficult it is. The universe is like a great golf hole that we are playing for the first time. The view from the tee box always looks much scarier than the hole really is. Change works the same way.

The flow of the cosmos allows us to leave our old ideas behind and replace them with new ones as we learn the errors of our ways. If our ideas were not evolving and we were trapped in a stagnant universe, then we would be unable to shed our mistakes. If we believe the same things when we die as we did when we were born, we have had no spiritual growth. It is this ever-changing mechanism that makes learning practical because it allows us to leave our mistakes in the past. It gives us continual new opportunities for a multitude of new experiences in each life. Change is inevitable and should be anticipated but never feared.

Diversity

When we look out the window we see cars, trees, animals, people and a vast array of objects. But the material diversity that we experience is merely a perception because everything is composed of a single substance. In order to teach us the nature of things, we are required to view the world as though everything is separate. This gives us a distorted perspective of reality but provides a convenient platform to set up differing experiences. Everything with which we interface reinforces the idea of multiplicity. For example, our brains take energy waves and create images of things that appear to be separate, like trees and animals. Our hands touch things that have different textures, and we taste things that have different flavors. But what we are really sensing are energy vibrations of varying amplitudes and frequencies. Our senses interpret these vibrations and present a diverse world to us.

To further enhance the diversity, things that are the same are valued differently to make them appear separate. Hot and cold are the same things, just different points on the scale. Fat and thin, tall and short, black and white, etc., are things that we use to try to differentiate. Even our sentences focus on things (nouns) not actions (verbs). Science is beginning to realize that all material objects are created out of a single building block, although it is still trying to decide exactly what that is. Our bodies and indeed everything within the universe are mostly empty space, but even when we get down to the atomic particles them-selves, Einstein showed us that matter and energy are equivalent with his formula $E=MC^2$ (where E=energy, M=mass, and C=speed of light). In other words, everything that we see and touch is just an energy form, including our bodies. Material diversity is part of the illusion.

However, the greatest illusion of diversity is us. Each of nature's enti-ties existing within the cosmos has at its core a spiritual being that is part of the divine self. This means that we are all part of one single enormous entity. We are all one! Every object in the cosmos is just a different aspect of a single spiritual entity, all with the single purpose of perfecting its soul, but each with a unique execution plan. The cosmos is an elaborate illusion that makes us believe that we are all separate, but we are not. "All is in The All and The All is in all."

THE ILLUSION OF FEAR

Of all the things that impede our spiritual growth, nothing comes close to fear. It causes us to cover up our past mistakes, avoid important lessons, and put unnecessary pressure on ourselves and others. We live in a world of fear because we don't realize our spirits cannot be harmed in any way except temporarily by our own poor decisions.

Fear is an emotion that can only be experienced in the natural realm; it is a key part of the illusion created for our benefit. We cannot understand the bliss of safety until we have experienced the lack thereof. However, experiencing fear is one thing, but letting it control our lives is something else. For many of us, fear causes irrational decisions; instead of seeing a challenge as it really is, we focus on the negative aspects to the exclusion of the path we know is right. Fear is a useful tool in our box of props, but like other emotions, it must be balanced and eventually conquered.

Fear plays upon our weaknesses and makes us more vulnerable as it draws the things that we fear to us. Our thoughts control our world and make things happen, and fearful thoughts are no exception[40]. Fear causes our vibratory energies to weaken, which makes us susceptible to more negative energies. Fear actually causes our fears to come true. We are capable of creating our own hells and sustaining them with amazing devotion, to the extent they become sovereign over our lives. The villains of the world have learned this long ago. When someone wants to impose his will on us, he begins by frightening us. Terrorists base their whole strategy on this concept. On a less violent scale, disreputable people use fear against the elderly and the poor. It is also the basis that many governments and religions use to maintain control of their people. Fear of the unknown is a classic tool of tyrants.

The problem with fear is it can become all consuming. It can cause us to run from our problems and cheat us out of the learning experiences that we need to execute our life plans. The best way to deal with our fears is to face them head-on. We need to understand the hold that our fears have on us and realize their superficial nature. Sometimes our fears are so dominant our life plans are based solely on dealing with them.

---

40 See chapter 7: Thought for more detail.

We need to recognize where those fears originated so we can understand that many of them were fabricated for the benefit of others.

FEAR OF DEATH

The fear of death is primarily attributed to religion. Most religions' main hold on their populations has always been through fear of suffering after death caused by God's wrath. The Western religions preach salvation if we comply with their teachings and endless suffering if we do not follow the church's doctrine. We are told that at death, Judgment Day determines how we exist in the afterlife. Of course, no one is perfect, so even the most devout people fear that their indiscretions, no matter how minor, may be cause enough for punishment. Those that have made major mistakes can be convinced that surely hell awaits them. Eastern religions threaten reincarnation into lower life forms and many more lives of suffering if their creed is not adhered to. Most religions preach creeds of fear, and they sell them as God's will, but there is no punishment waiting for any of us, and no religion has a divine charter. The world is just and we only get the experiences that we need in order to learn our lessons. Once that occurs, then the matter is forgotten. Fearing death is nonsense.

In a lesser way, science also contributes to our fear of death, because it claims that we go out of existence when we die. As such, some non-religious people fear death because they are not ready to stop existing. We yearn for immortality of the flesh because it is all some scientifically oriented people know, but this makes no sense either. We need to realize that science has focused its attention on the physical world and has yet to discover the transcendent force behind the cosmos; it has focused on the cave wall shadows, not the light source behind.

We do leave the physical world at death, but only temporarily. We return to our natural spiritual state until we are ready to return to the natural realm for another set of experiences. When we realize that God does not support any religion, we are his children, and we are always in his good graces no matter how foolishly we act, then death can have no hold on us.

FEAR OF SUFFERING

Pain and suffering in this lifetime are concerns for everyone. Disease is usually our biggest fear, whether it is cancer, heart failure, Alzheimer's, etc. Continually dwelling on the idea of getting a disease helps bring it to us and even adds to its severity. Like all objects within a mind, disease is a thought. Our bodies follow our minds, and if we think about something all the time, we end up attracting it. If we do get a disease, the key to a cure is to embrace our sickness, knowing we got the disease so we could learn something that would help us align ourselves with God. We need to love the sickness because it is helping us grow; shed the fear, which is aggravating the problem, and then *believe in the cure*.

Fear of crime is especially prevalent among the elderly and those living in high-felony areas. Like disease, crime is attracted to those that fear it. When crime strikes us, then we need to embrace the crime as a lesson in life. We reap what we sow; so if it occurs, then accept the experience for what it is and move on.

Accidents and natural disasters are simply part of our life plans and when we are affected by them then we are simply learning lessons. These lessons can be difficult, but fearing them only increases their difficulty. Again, accept them as part of life and move on.

Fear of losing a loved one can be one of the most difficult fears of all, but when it happens we need to realize that our loved ones are just moving on, as their work in this life has come to an end. When we die, those that we care the most about will be there to greet us upon our arrival and will surely participate in our future adventures. Similarly, divorce and breaking up with someone we cherish is always difficult, but when it happens, we need to realize we are both moving on due to the fact that our work in each other's lives has come to an end and served its purpose. In both cases we should be glad for our loved ones, as they have met their obligations, and be thankful for all the help they gave us while they were here.

FEAR OF MATERIAL LOSS

Our material focus has totally distorted our view of what is important. Obtaining material objects and honors is considered the ultimate culmination of our lives' work, but it is the lessons we learn along the way and take with us into eternity that are really important. When we lose our material wealth or adoration from others, then that is the lesson at hand. Deal with it with integrity and accept it for what it is: a valuable opportunity to learn how it feels to have lost something you prize; then move on.

FEAR OF FAILURE

Fear of failure is a two-edged sword. Few of us have not pushed ourselves a little harder because we did not want to fail. This fear can aid us in our experiences as we take our tasks to heart, and when the experiences conclude we will have gotten the most out of them because we put the most into them. It is when the fear of failure incapacitates us that it becomes a problem. We get ourselves tied up with the images we portray to the world, and then we fear we cannot live up to them, so we either stop trying or make poor decisions. We need to remember that our mistakes are what teach us right from wrong.

Many of us have self-confidence problems that make us fear not being worthy. We fear we are not able to succeed either at work, in sports, at school, or even in our relationships. Sometimes we even fear others will find out we are not worthy of their love. But each of us is a god in the making. A day will come when no one living on this earth will be as capable as we are at anything because our understanding will exceed all the wisdom presently on earth today. Within each of us is the divine spark that is blossoming into a unique and valuable spirit. We are all one, and we are no better or no worse than anyone else. We are all deserving of everyone's love, including God's.

We need to realize that the whole concept of failure is an illusion. We are here to learn, not to succeed in some material pursuit. Failure is no more than a hard lesson. There is no such thing as failing in the spiritual realm because we learn from all our experiences, and we learn the most from our biggest mistakes.

FEAR CAN CONTROL OUR LIVES

Fear controls us when we let it take over our psyches. It can even make a difficult situation worse by attracting more negative energy to us and thereby accelerating a disease or worsening a catastrophe. In this circumstance it acts like positive feedback in which the fear actually makes the matter worse. Mind over matter has many subtle implications, and letting fear unduly influence our lives is an important one.

Insecurity, which is the fear of being inadequate, lies at the source of much of our overindulgence. Repressed bad experiences from either this life or, more probably, past lives cause us to have distorted views of ourselves and life in general. We might overeat to compensate for fear of experiencing past-life deprivation, or we might overdose on drugs or alcohol for fear of facing our problems. Whatever the cause, our indulgences are rooted in fear. The extreme example of this is panic attacks, which arise when fears take over our rational minds. It may be a single fear or an accumulation of multiple fears that overcomes us; whatever the cause, this irrational feeling can be all consuming.

FEAR CAUSES SELFISHNESS

Despite how easy selflessness is to understand and how universally deplored selfishness is, mankind still has a very difficult time adhering to selfless behavior. Although most people across the globe are basically good, our self-interests make it very difficult to raise our standards and continuously put others above ourselves.

If we stop being so selfish, then others will not be able to intimidate or take advantage of us. Fretting over promotions and financing bigger homes, and struggling with other signs of our successes are all self-inflicted fears that cause us totally unnecessary stress. They are the penalties that we pay for our materialistic perspective. Fear is the biggest driver of selfish behavior. It is our many fears of failure, death, etc., that cause us to act in irrational ways. Once we understand that we live in a safe world and fear is an illusion, then living a selfless life will be much easier.

CONQUERING OUR FEARS

Fear is helpful as an aid in learning our lessons. Everyone has a certain level of fear in normal life, which is fine. It is when fear becomes an irrational part of our decision-making processes that we need to deal with it.

Fear is a futuristic event. No one ever fears the present or the past; it is only the unknown future that we fear. We fear uncertainty. We need to keep in mind that our planned lessons will occur no matter what we do, so it makes no sense to worry about them. When fears occur, staying positive and dealing with them courageously is the best approach. A strong mind can readily resolve even the worst situations if it dwells on the positives instead of the negatives.

We should set up realistic expectations for ourselves and not get overly discouraged by our apparent shortfalls. Life is not a competition; it is truly irrelevant what others learn or what props they need to have to learn their lessons. We must realize that our accomplishments and social status have no importance in the afterlife. We are all on a journey toward perfection where no one wins and no one loses.

Fear can be conquered over time by realizing our lives have a purpose and meaning. We exist in a safe place where no harm can reach us. We are in a cocoon, sheltered and controlled by the Universal Consciousness. Our every step is monitored and supported by those who have only our best interests at heart, and it is in our best interests to overcome the illusions of danger.

Franklin D. Roosevelt was right when he said there is nothing to fear but fear itself. We have put ourselves in this world and established the life plans we need to exercise. The plans surely have difficult lessons for us to learn, but they provide benefits for our good choices. No one is ever given an experience that he or she is not capable of handling. We must accept life as being just a play, and we are the actors. No spirit ever really gets hurt in life, no matter what suffering happens to the body; it just looks like it in the play. At death the pain goes away, and we return to the spiritual realm and get ready for the next act. We all come back in the next scene wiser, stronger, and in more important roles.

CHANGING FEAR INTO AWARENESS

We live in a world that on a superficial basis appears chaotic, irrational, arbitrary, meaningless, and filled with evil, but this is all an illusion caused by so many divergent life plans operating simultaneously. The cosmos is completely organized and running near perfection. There is no doubt bad things are happening around the globe, and our news media is quick to point them out, but life deals out difficult lessons only where they are merited and only to those who will learn needed lessons from them. If our own little worlds seem out of control, then that is our fault and our problem to resolve. It is not the cosmos that needs correction; it is us.

Our attitude sets up certain vibration levels. A positive attitude allows us to receive positive energy, which is healing; but negative attitudes prevent us from receiving these energies. A weak vibrational field encourages disease, poor intellectual arguments, lack of focus, and a generally stressful life. A normal, well-adjusted person is better protected from these extremes.

Compatible energy patterns allow us to develop friendships, but as we each grow differently, incompatible energy patterns can make us turn away from people we have known for years. It is best to surround ourselves with the people whose energy patterns reinforce the positives in our lives and move away from the negative influences. We can only help people who want to be helped.

Self-restraint is the most effective regulator of the body's energies. Those of us addicted to certain negative patterns constantly battle neuroses and bad health, and we more easily get involved with false dogmas and other fearful situations. When our lives are balanced, then it is less likely our mistakes will result in extremely stressful situations. We will still experience the lesson, and we may make mistakes, but the resulting karma will be easier to handle. Obsessive behavior can cause us to become gullible and compulsively pursue material gains, which opens us up to even more trouble. Self-restraint is a great ally.

A word of caution: the personality is both introverted and extroverted. Our introverted personality is who we really are with all our flaws. We show that only to those very close to us and maybe to nobody at all. Our extroverted personality is what we show to the world, and it is a cover-up mechanism for our self-perceived weaknesses. If we allow our extroverted personality to dominate us to the extent that we never let ourselves be the introvert that we really are, then we risk becoming a shell and the introverted man shrivels. We need to recognize and accept our weaknesses so we can work on them, because when we try to hide our faults they can morph into much greater problems.

The Old Testament and Torah are erroneous documents in that they go on and on about how God will punish us if we displease him, but none of this is true. God is unbelievably loving, and none of these terrible threats have any basis in truth. He only has our best interests at heart. He understands our weaknesses and has long since overcome any feeling of anger or intolerance for some foolish thing we have done. He only wants two things from us: our love, and our effort toward improving ourselves. Fear of God is a myth conceived to encourage us to follow certain doctrines, and nothing more.

Contentment starts from respecting ourselves enough to not always need to be the first in line or the best dressed or the most outspoken. Remember, we are diamonds in the rough, gods in the making, yet we must not take ourselves too seriously. We are not perfect, and we never will be, but that is OK. We are not expected to be perfect, only to improve. The greatest gift we can give ourselves is to learn to laugh at our mistakes. We all do foolish things in our humble efforts to climb the ladder of wisdom and understanding. Failure is simply coming up short of our personal expectations. So what? It simply is not that big a deal. Time is on our side; we have eternity to get it right. If we just do the best we can this time around by taking one baby step at a time, we will soon be surprised at how far we have traveled. We should enjoy life and marvel at the wonders of ourselves. The universe would not be the same without us.

Fear is a phantom that can only touch us if we allow it!

LEARNING IN THE ILLUSION

The illusion provides an effective method of learning by: (1) teaching from the particulars and expanding into the general principles, (2) helping us focus on mistakes, and (3) teaching us about ourselves.

Particular to General

Truth is incredibly complex, especially emotional truth, so each experience can only teach us a small aspect of what we need to learn about any given situation. Each lesson, when added to many other lessons, begins to give us a perspective of the general principle we are trying to understand.

Every spirit that has reached a level capable of incarnating into a human body has achieved a minimum level of knowledge. We may believe far more opinion than truth, and we may be heavily biased toward the material illusion, but we are all able to function within a sophisticated society at least to some level. We have achieved this through a long process of being exposed to multiple sides of many general principles.

The process of understanding goes from learning a myriad of particular aspects of an issue to the general principle. This is familiar to us as it corresponds to how we learn at work or at school. We start out learning the fundamentals, like adding and subtracting, and then work our way up to the more general principles and laws of physics and chemistry. We go from the particulars to the general. Our life plans work the same way. We must have mastery of the lesser concepts in order to have mastery over the greater principles. However, if we do not get the particulars right, then the conclusions that we draw about the general principles will be wrong. We see a good example of this when we look at how astronomy has viewed the cosmos. For the longest time, the stars and universe were viewed as stationary. Then Edwin Hubble, the famed astronomer, discovered that the universe was expanding as all the galaxies were moving away from each other. This led to the big bang theory, which surprised everyone but soon became a general principle of astronomy. A few years ago, astronomers discovered that the cosmos was not only expanding, but the expansion was accelerating, which changed the big bang theory. The point is that as we find additional particulars, we need to change our general principles.

It takes a great many experiences to fully grasp even one of life's truths. God understands that wisdom comes to us gradually as we slowly get the universal principles correct. He painstakingly teaches us one particular after another until we can see the general principle, and then he painstakingly corrects any misconceptions that we might still have with additional lessons. When God is done teaching us the lessons, we fully understand the principles of concern. This is the crux of why we need so many lives to fully understand truth. There are many truths to learn, and each truth has a multitude of subtle aspects.

The purpose of the life plan is to afford us the opportunity to have certain experiences, but we might only learn part of the lesson or, conceivably, nothing at all. Sometimes we are so biased in a single perspective that it takes many lessons to break our hold on a misconception. The longer we persist and the harder that we grasp at old ideas, the more difficult it will be to finally jolt us out of our errant ways. This is especially true when we have based an entire belief system on a false concept. Also, we have freedom of choice, so we can ignore the lesson or even change the experience if we so choose. We will always learn something from every experience, but maybe not the intended lesson.

Mistakes

We learn far more from our mistakes than our successes. The bigger the mistake, the more we learn from it. Our hardships are our best experiences because we become emotionally involved with the details. Hardship captures our attention, focuses our minds on the issues, and leads us into introspection. When things go well, we seldom know why. We give ourselves undue credit for wise decisions when more likely the circumstances were simply not lessons we needed to learn at the time. When we realize we learn more from our mistakes than our successes, it is easier to accept our mistakes and even embrace our failures.

If we are going to accept our own failures, then we need to accept the failures of others as well. We have been taught that failure is a bad thing, and we look down on other people's mistakes. If we insist on judging others, which is never a good idea, it should be on the evolution of their ideas, not on their previous positions.

Our Role in the Illusion

Each of us is a key part of the illusion. Although we appear to be insignificant physical beings in an immense universe, in reality, we are spirits having life experiences in a universe made for our benefit. Most importantly, our spirits were created in the image of the Universal Consciousness. As such, if we can learn about ourselves, then we will also learn about the Universal Consciousness. We are far more important than we appear to be.

Each person's world is a reflection of his or her own thoughts and beliefs. What we think, how we approach our problems, the people we interface with, and every aspect of our lives are reflections of how we think. We modify the universe in a small but significant way by building a world around us that fits with our inner desires and needs. Since our world is a reflection of us, our experiences inherently teach us about ourselves. We create circumstances, react to them, and in the process learn about ourselves.

Our lessons use other spiritual beings to provide us with the feelings that our life plans require. The specific circumstances that created those feelings are of little importance. What is important is the feelings we get and how we react to those feelings. We are the only ones who understand our reactions, because we are the only ones that know the whys of our motives.

Our spirits are microcosms of the Universal Consciousness, so we are able to learn about it by learning about ourselves. When we find ourselves in a circumstance that makes us feel bad, we can know that if the Universal Consciousness were in the same circumstance, it would also feel bad. Of course, it would never be in that circumstance because it has gone far beyond us, but the point is that its feelings would be the same as our feelings if it had the same wisdom. When we learn about ourselves, we are also learning about the Universal Consciousness , and in doing so we are able to grow into higher planes of consciousness.

ASPECTS OF LEARNING

The illusion purposely puts obstacles in our way for us to overcome. Some of our most difficult circumstances arise where we are heavily influenced by people that have power over us, such as government leaders, religious leaders, and supervisors. It is important to resist the temptation to buckle under and go with the powers that be when we know their influence is wrong. We don't need to stand up and get run over, but we need to persist in doing the right thing, or else we will get swept up in the tides of omission or commission. In the end, the path toward making the right decisions comes from reason and courage; it is only the illusion that makes us believe wrong decisions will make life easier.

We need to embrace our rivals and even our enemies, as they play an important part in our illusion. By taking the opposing position, our antagonists are doing our bidding for us. They force us to deal with various aspects of an issue we might otherwise not see. We are all in this together, and our adversaries are every bit as important as our friends.

Memory is energy, and a bad memory is negative energy. We would be better off viewing our bad memories as difficult lessons that we created for ourselves and realizing that they were actually positive learning experiences. Stressing over bad memories and feeling remorse and guilt impedes our growth by drawing negative energy to us. We need to accept past mistakes as being positive experiences and learn to forgive and forget.

RECOGNIZING TRUTH WITHIN THE ILLUSION

Truth is hard to filter out from the background noise within the illusion, but it is always available to those who seek it. Truth is not the social, historical, and scientific opinions that are taught in our schools and universities. Unfortunately, much of what passes for truth is opinion sanctified by tradition.

Truth exists in all that we see, but discernment and discrimination are needed to discover it. Everyone offers a level of wisdom, both the fools and the wise. Some people seem to make better choices and appear better balanced. They are not driven to extremes, yet they remain earnest and energetic and live with more inner peace and happiness. They don't strive for recognition but are successful in their endeavors. Life just seems to work well for them. These are the ones that have gained enough wisdom to handle the lives they lead. We all have different elements of knowledge that we have accumulated over the eons. Allowing others to share their wisdom with us is of great value.

Knowing what is not true can be a great step toward finding truth. If we can eliminate some of the false choices, it will keep us from heading down wrong paths. Our journey does not require an optimal direction; it only requires continual progress.

Although complete wisdom and understanding are in our future, at our stage of development we cannot hope to know the how and why of the Universal Consciousness; our focus needs to be on what truth is. By strengthening our souls' attributes and characteristics we will be able to increase our discernment of truth. Truth is like an onion, where every layer evokes ever more questions. Nothing is black-and-white; everything is gray. Spiritual growth is measured by our ability to discern ever finer shades of gray.

IMPORTANCE OF ILLUSION

Buddhism teaches that ignorance is a condition from which all other miseries originate and ties us to this realm. Wisdom opens the door and frees us from these bonds, but wisdom is only perceived through first-hand experiences. Others can tell us about their experience, but until we go through it ourselves, we cannot fully understand it. We will only know how others feel when the tables are turned and we see circumstances from their perspectives. We need to have the feelings of the emotions imprinted on our souls to fully appreciate the impact of the lesson.

Wisdom needs to be learned slowly and completely. For that reason, the divine will, love, and reason are embedded in all things yet hidden from mankind by the veils of illusions so that we can slowly experience them. When we realize truth we will know what is real and what is illusion. When we attain wisdom we will know how truth and the illusion work together.

The search for truth is the search to understand God and his realm, which begins by learning about us. It is the growth of our souls that continuously demands ever greater and more diligent pursuits of wisdom and understanding. By doing this we continually become more worthy of God's trust and earn ever-greater freedom. This newfound freedom allows us greater flexibility on our journeys, but the goal of perfection is always the only aspiration.

Manly P. Hall noted that *the seeker of wisdom comes gradually to realize that he exists only because of the wisdom that he seeks, and the wisdom sought for exists only because it is sought.* God created wisdom, and then he created us so that we could learn it. It is the illusion that allows us to seek.

CHAPTER 7

THOUGHT

Our life is shaped by our mind; we become
what we think. Suffering follows an
evil thought like the wheels of a cart
that follow the oxen that pull it.

Our life is shaped by our mind; we become
what we think. Joy follows a pure
thought like a shadow that never leaves.

– The Dhammapada[41]

Key Concept:	*Thought is the all-powerful force that allows us to evolve into ever-higher beings.*

THE NATURE OF THOUGHT

What are thoughts? They seem so elusive and insubstantial. Thoughts seem to pass through our minds in a blink of an eye. We don't know where they come from, and we don't know where they go. We can recall them or we can forget them. They appear fleeting and inconsequential,

---

41 The Dhammapada is a Buddhist scripture that is composed of sayings attributed to Buddha and written in verse form.

but yet they determine how we feel and shape our views on everything and everyone with which we come in contact. They determine if we are happy or sad and cause us to get or lose a job, fall in or out of love, have friends, and communicate with others. When we think about it, our thoughts are really the most important thing we have; in fact, they are the only thing we have!

We view ourselves as physical bodies controlled by physical brains, so it is natural for us to view physical objects as the real world; but physical objects have no real substance or lasting value. They only give the illusion of reality because we view them from a material perspective. The fragility of physical objects can be seen in their very limited existence: our homes last fifty to one hundred years, our clothes last five to ten years, and fresh food lasts days. Even our solar system will only last about ten billion years, which seems like a long time to us, but it is only a blink of an eye when compared to eternity. The cosmos is temporal and has no lasting value in its own right.

On the other hand, thoughts are the only things spiritual beings value because they are real and everlasting. Although thoughts appear to leave us when our attention is changed, they never do. Once we have a thought, it is with us forever and becomes part of our nature. Thoughts allow us to understand truth and add to our souls, so we become more than we were. A thought might be insignificant, or it might be a keystone that we build our future lives on, but in either case it remains with us forever. Thoughts are the only things of importance to a mind, because like a mind, they too are eternal.

Thought is a Force

Thoughts are like physical objects, since both are composed of energy. Like a physical object, an individual thought consists of an energy packet with its own unique frequency signature. However, unlike material energy, which only retains its form for a short period of time, thoughts are permanent

Physics tells us that a field consists of particles held together by an electromagnetic force. Metaphysics says this force is thought. If this is true, then the four known forces (the electromagnetic force, the strong and weak nuclear forces, and gravity) would all be different aspects of and subject to the thought force. It appears thought functions in the same way as both light and matter in that all three exhibit dual properties. They each radiate like a wave and travel as discrete packets like a photon or electron. Even quantum mechanics says that it is thought (an observer) that collapses Schrödinger's particle waveform[42] equation, resulting in changing the probability of an electron into becoming an actual particle of matter.

In the natural realm, atoms and molecules are the building blocks of our bodies and other material objects. Similarly, in the spiritual realm, thoughts are the building blocks for our spirits. Although the essence of all spirits is fundamentally the same, each spirit has its own look about it since each one consists of a unique collection of ideas. The brighter and whiter a spirit appears, the wiser it is.

Thought Controls Matter

Both physics and psychology have independently found strong evidence that thought influences matter, and it appears to do so from the minutest to the grandest scale throughout the material universe. There have been numerous studies over the last one hundred years showing that thought influences physical events. This is part of a general area of psychic phenomena (sometimes referred to as the Greek letter psi) known as psychokinesis (PK), in which a person is able to physically alter an object through the use of only his thoughts. Robert Jahn and

---

42 David Bohm, *Quantum Theory*, p 191-2

Brenda Dunne[43] have done extremely interesting work at the Princeton Engineering Anomalies Research laboratory (PEAR), where they have demonstrated time and time again that if a person throwing dice concentrates on the outcome of the throw, the results are statistically biased toward the number being targeted. They found the results of studies conducted over very large numbers of events were statistically skewed such that it would be astronomically rare for such an outcome to occur naturally. Even more interesting is that some tests were done with supposedly random electronic number generators, and they produced the same biased results as manual events. They also showed that the influencer could be local or from a remote location, even thousands of miles away.

In his book *The Conscious Universe*, Dean Radin reports on various tests of dice throws that have been done over the last century, where virtually hundreds of thousands of data points have been taken by numerous investigators. The results consistently showed that when the thrower concentrated on a particular outcome, the results were heavily skewed in favor of the desired number. One such analysis looked at ninety-six independent tests between 1935 an 1987 and showed that the outcomes were skewed in favor of mind influencing matter such that the odds of those results occurring naturally were three million to one, instead of what would normally be expected to be an even distribution.

Nonscientific examples of PK, using only one's mind to cure disease, bend spoons, or perform superhuman feats of strength under extreme conditions, are commonplace. Although science struggles with these claims because so few of them are repeatable, there are too many

---

43 Robert G. Jahn is professor of aerospace sciences and dean emeritus of Princeton University's School of Engineering and Applied Science, founder and director of the PEAR laboratory, and chairman of International Consciousness Research Laboratory (ICRL). Brenda J. Dunne holds degrees in psychology and the humanities, was the manager of the PEAR laboratory from its inception in 1979, and was president of ICRL.

instances to ignore. These examples need to be taken more seriously, because not everyone reporting an event is trying to deceive us.

There is a huge body of work that supports PK phenomena that has been done throughout the years and around the globe. Numerous scientific studies and nonscientific instances have taken place over the last century; these have demonstrated the phenomena of mind influencing matter to be a reality. How this works is only speculation.

Thought Created the Cosmos

Logic tells us the universe could not exist unless some transcendent power outside of the space-time continuum created it. A self-created material universe populated by rational beings who are created at birth and whose self-awareness is based on chemical reactions is hard to comprehend. It is much easier for me to understand the organization and interdependence of the cosmos if an intelligent mind is behind it. If the universe as we see it had always existed from the beginning of eternity, it would have slowly but surely ceased to exist eons ago as the stars and galaxies slowly ran out of energy. There would be no energy available for a big bang to happen. There has never been a single rational argument put forth for how the universe could ever have occurred on its own.

From a rational perspective, the inescapable conclusion is that a transcendent power, which I call the Universal Consciousness, created the universe. If the Universal Consciousness is a mind, then it stands to reason that the force that it would use to create the universe would be thought. When we think about it, the only force we could conceive of as being capable of creating the universe is thought. It is interesting that Genesis, ancient Hinduism (the Upanishads), and mystic philosophies all agree that God's mind is the power behind the universe. It follows that God must be continuing to maintain it, otherwise the cosmos would return to its unorganized state of chaos in a short period of time.

The cosmos is highly organized, continually changing, and filled with interdependent systems. To me, it is inconceivable that this occurred naturally. Thought is not only the greatest force in existence, it is the only force in existence, because all the other forces are derived from it. Thought is the transcendent force that created and continues to control the universe. The cosmos could not exist if it was not for thought.

Limitation of Thought

After reviewing the available data,[44] I cannot postulate any rational conclusion other than a mind can and does influence matter through the application of a thought force. Despite the large database of controlled experiments clearly showing the direct relationship between thought and matter, this concept is one of the most difficult aspects of reality for most of us to grasp. The problem we have is that our thoughts and wishes don't seem to be consistent with our day-to-day experiences. The reasons we cannot go to Las Vegas and see a one-to-one correspondence to our wishes are fourfold:

1. Our powers of concentration are not as strong as they need to be. At our level of maturity, our thoughts impact matter, but rarely do they suddenly and dramatically alter it.

2. Our minds are not properly focused. We may hope for a good outcome, but our minds are all over the place and our thoughts become scattered. If we want the dice to act a certain way, we need to have an extremely high level of concentration.

3. Self-doubt is a killer. Any doubt sends a confusing message to the material object.

---

44 For example, Michael Schmicker's *Best Evidence* identifies several areas of psi in which a good deal of evidence has been collected that confirm positive PK results. Studies like these are far more common than most of us realize.

4. Most importantly, the Universal Consciousness created and controls the cosmos with its mind, so it's extremely powerful thoughts already influence the behavior of the dice.

The Universal Consciousness has established the physical laws of nature and set the events that we view as the world around us in motion with its own mind. For us to alter those events and change the world to our liking, we need to first overcome nature's intentions. We are allowed to do this; however, at our level we can only control small areas, i.e., our own little worlds. If the Universal Consciousness were not already influencing the same matter that we are trying to influence, then it would be much easier for us to do it.

How thought controls matter is an open issue. David Bohm speculated that matter has a conscious element inherent in its nature. This may be true, but it could also be that since matter and thought are both vibratory energies, thoughts cause matter to resonate in a certain way and subsequently influence its behavior. When thoughts are at the correct frequency and amplitude, they are capable of resonating with matter and influencing it. This might explain why our thoughts' impact on matter does not appear to be that strong much of the time. As we become wiser and strengthen and focus our minds, our thoughts will be stronger and our impact on matter will become more apparent. Anyone who studies the multitude of phenomena in these various fields will not have a hard time convincing themselves of the validity of mind over matter, but it may be a while before science catches up with a complete theory of it, as skeptics prevail.

THOUGHT COMMUNICATION

Since a thought wave is radiated energy, if it is strong enough it can be received over a wide area by anyone that is tuned to it. Most of our thoughts are not intense enough or well-focused enough to travel long distances. But thought communication between people of like mind, especially in close proximity, is very common, and it happens most often between people that know each other well. Most of us have had an experience in which we were thinking about something, and out of the blue, someone near us spoke up on the same subject. This also happens at greater distances, but we rarely learn about it.

Thought communication can be seen throughout history when we realize that ideas have their time. Highly focused thought waves generated by extremely enthusiastic people—or better yet, focused groups—can be received by minds that are receptive to those particular thoughts if they have sympathetic vibratory resonances, even when they are far away. When a society reaches a certain state of maturity, it produces a number of minds that are capable of entertaining certain new ideas. This is seen when technical breakthroughs happen nearly simultaneously across the globe although no physical contact has taken place. For example, at the same time Wilber and Orville Wright were building the first airplane in North Carolina, the same thing was happening in Germany and India. Radar was developed simultaneously in the 1930s in Germany, Great Britain, Japan, and the United States. Newton and Leibniz both discovered calculus at about the same time. Charles Darwin and Alfred Russel Wallace both discovered evolution, apparently independently. Three mathematicians independently invented decimal fractions. Oxygen was discovered by Joseph Priestley in Wiltshire in 1774 and by Carl Wilhelm Scheele in Uppsala a year earlier. Color photography was invented at the same time by Charles Cros and Louis Arthur Ducos du Hauron in France. Logarithms were invented by John Napier and Henry Briggs in Britain, and by Joost Bürgi in Switzerland. Ogburn and Thomas note that there were four independent discoveries of sunspots, all in 1611; namely, by Galileo in Italy, Scheiner in Germany, Fabricius in Holland, and Harriott in England, and the law of the conservation of energy, so significant in science and philosophy, was formulated four times independently in 1847, by Joule, Thomson, Colding and Helmholz. There seem to have been at least six different inventors of the thermometer and no less than nine claimants of the invention of the telescope. Typewriting machines were invented simultaneously in England and in America by several individuals in these countries. The steamboat is claimed as the "exclusive" discovery of, individually, Fulton, Jouffroy, Rumsey, Stevens, and Symmington[45]. One could argue that society develops an infrastructure that produces these ideas and the products are an obvious outcome. But with such disparate societies and so many examples so close together in time, it is hard to conceive that it was the underlying social structure and not the genius of individual thought that caused the coincidences. Ideas have their time, and with endless examples simultaneous inventions are unlikely to be chance.

What we refer to as extrasensory perception (ESP) is simply thought waves used in a controlled manner. There are a number of areas in which our thoughts allow us to communicate in unusual ways. Remote viewing is a fascinating subject that has been actively studied for at least one hundred years by both governments and universities. The US Army's Star Gate program from 1972 to 1995 continually demonstrated that certain individuals were capable of visualizing and describing activities taking place in real time in remote areas with which they were totally unfamiliar. The US government did this in response to similar efforts by the USSR, and although this particular research effort has ended, there is reason to believe that subsequent programs are now going on around the globe. Also, PEAR laboratory has been doing research on thought communication since 1979 with remarkable results. Details on this can be easily found in books and on the web. Joseph McMoneagle's, *Remote Viewing Secrets*, is a good book regarding this subject.

---

45 All of these examples were taken from Wikipedia and many more can be easily found on the Internet.,

THOUGHTS CHANGE OUR LIVES

Thoughts not only control material objects, they also control the world around us. The cosmos functions like a living organism, existing for our educational benefit and adapting to our needs. The Universal Consciousness allows us to locally influence and change our corners of the universe to fit our needs. If we want to improve our lives, the power and resources to do it reside within us. We have the ability to change the cosmos because our minds are part of the Universal Consciousness. We can only impact a small piece of the universe, but those changes can have a big impact on our lives and enable us to build our own worlds and live out our life plans. It is especially important to change our lives if we don't like who we have become or where our lives are headed. If we are basically living happy and contented lives, then we are probably following our life plans and no major alterations are necessary. However, if life is not progressing well and we seem to be on endless treadmills, then change is needed, as we have somehow gotten off track. Life is like riding a raft down a river; we will eventually arrive at the mouth no matter what we do, but how we steer the raft will have a large impact on how well the trip goes. How we steer the raft will not have much impact on the river, but it can have a significant impact on us.

Commit

Changing our lives takes more than wanting change or wishing for it to happen; it takes committing to it. It requires deciding what we want, focusing our attention on it, believing we can achieve it, and then acting upon it. Our minds can only control matter when we send them unmistakable and continual directives. Our minds control the world we live in, so a wishy-washy mind creates a wishy-washy world. Aspiration, focus, commitment, and a strong sense of purpose are needed for improving our lives.

By relentlessly directing our thoughts on a goal and working hard toward achieving it, the barriers begin to subside and the world reforms and molds into a place better suited to meet our needs. Our thoughts actually change the circumstances of our lives. It could be educating ourselves, breaking bad habits, succeeding in work or school, getting healthier, or anything else we desire. We can create whole new worlds for ourselves by simply refocusing our thoughts and making different decisions. It is not just we who change, the world around us changes as well. In short, thought is the power that allows us to be the masters of our own destinies.

Process

It might help to appreciate how this process works by imagining a master artist trying to instruct his students on the finer aspects of painting. In order to demonstrate what a beautiful painting looks like, he creates a true masterpiece painted on a gigantic canvas. Each student is allocated a very small section of the painting in which he or she can modify the artist's work. The artist insists that the students use his original artwork as a guide and only make small changes until they get the hang of it, and then they are given more leeway. The student's mistakes do not concern the master, because the more they practice the better they get, and besides, he can always paint over anything he doesn't like when the students are done. But because the artist only has one canvas and likes to paint, he continuously revises the picture, concentrating on areas where the students are not painting or have finished. As such, the painting is never completed, and the scene is always changing. Now envision the canvas as the cosmos, the elements that make up the cosmos as the paint, the artist as the Universal Consciousness, the students as the incarnated spirits, and the brushes as all their creative thoughts. The areas that the students are allowed to change are what we would consider to be their own little worlds. A spirit can change his piece of the cosmos as he likes, as long as he stays within the structure of the universe. In other words, we have certain guidelines, but in time, as we develop a better understanding of the process, we will be given more freedom and control over our actions. Like the students with the painting, our purpose here is to learn.

Whatever we aspire to will slowly come to us if we make the effort to attain it. It is not so much that we need to go get these things as we need to attract them to us. We do this by training our minds to be more receptive to better things. If our minds cannot resonate at the correct frequencies, then we will not be able to take advantage of these opportunities, which are always present but not always within our reach. Thought changes us by allowing us to take advantage of new opportunities. We need to make ourselves receptive to the positive things in life and resistant to the negative things.

Vision

It is critical to have the big picture in mind to start a process of change; we need to know what we want to change or what we want to become. If we create an image of how we want things to be at some point in time, then it will provide us with a tangible end result that we can pursue. For example, we might decide we want a better life for our children, including a nicer home, better car, better food and clothing, and a good education. This will be the goal, so we must continually picture ourselves and our families in those circumstances. Don't think of it as a dream: it is a goal we are committed to achieving, and visualizing it helps make it happen.

Parsing the Problem

After visualizing, we need to start building the foundations for our goals. We do this by breaking the problem down into bite-size pieces on which we can work. If we feel we need a better-paying job to fund a new lifestyle, then we need to prepare for it by starting to do better in the job we presently have; better pay requires better performance. We must take more responsibility, increase the quality and quantity of our work, dress better, be on time, cooperate with others, be a team player, keep a positive attitude, and basically be the best employee possible. If we want a better job, we need to start learning how to be a more valuable employee. Then we must look beyond that job to better understand our aspirations. This may require different training and/or more education, so we need to decide what is needed and pursue it. If we want a nicer house, then we need to get used to living in a nicer home by fixing up our present one. If it is a mess, clean it up. If it needs repair or renovation, get started. This does not necessarily require money, but it does require effort. If we want a better home, we need to raise our expectations for our living conditions. Life requires aspiration and effort. The same process should be used to improve our health, relationships, and anything that we want to change. We need to strengthen our foundation so we are ready for new things.

Deal with the Result

The catch to all this is that we must accept the consequences that go along with our decisions, so we need to think them through before we commit. Getting what we strive for is really pretty simple, but getting what we really need is not as easy. Dealing with what goes along with our wishes can be very difficult if we make the wrong choices. When we create new paths for our lives, we need to really analyze what we want to change. This is more difficult than it sounds.

For example, concentrating our thoughts on getting a job may sound like a good idea if we have been unemployed a long time, but you may not want to wash windows or sling burgers if you have a degree in chemistry so you need to be more specific. A nebulous focus will get a nebulous response. We need to be specific in focusing on a well-paid job, good working conditions, challenging tasks, etc. If we don't like what appears, then we can always turn it down and try again. No one in the spiritual world will be insulted, nor will they really care, as these are our lives to do with as we see fit.

We are the ones changing our world, and we have the right to change it any way we want; but if we get a good opportunity and turn it down, and then continue wishing for more, it might tell us something about ourselves. We may not know what we want or be ready to handle the responsibility that goes with the opportunity. If we want to improve our situations in life we need to be honest with ourselves. We can fool others, but we cannot fool ourselves. We also need to keep our focus within the realm of our capabilities. Wanting to be the president of the United States is probably not practical for most of us, because we do not have the resident qualifications or time line to get them, especially if we are not very young. The grander the desire, the harder the work that is needed to get there and the longer it will take. Persistence and self-confidence are necessary, and focusing on the next rung of the ladder is the most practical approach, but aspirations that are too high are far better than too low.

Big changes require us to start new in some aspect of our lives, like getting another job. There are two ways to leave a job, from a position of strength or a position of weakness. It is easy to decide to leave from weakness when our jobs or our lives are not going well or we have been let go, but in those cases our self-confidence is usually damaged, so success in the new position is more difficult, although certainly not impossible. Leaving from a position of strength is a harder choice because we are considered successful and looked up to by our peers, but our self-confidence is in place, which aides our success going forward. It is always better to leave from a position of strength because self-confident thoughts are so powerful that success in the new position will be easier.

In either case, change is for the better and should not be feared. We need to look at these changes as giving us opportunities to work on another piece of our life plans.

Selflessness

Changes that benefit others will surely have the best outcomes. Greed and selfishness create karma, so we may get what we ask for but it might not be what we want in the long run. Focusing on a life of helping others, gaining wisdom, and improving ourselves is the best strategy. In fact, focusing on a life in which we burn off karma would be as good as anything. At first it might seem that things don't go our way, but if we face life selflessly, when it is all over we will probably be very happy with the results, and that happiness will last long into the future.

Responsibility

It is important to take responsibility for executing our life plans, which inevitably requires change as we move from one circumstance to the next. If we have the courage to follow our instincts, we will find ourselves following that plan, but fear and indecision can interfere with our execution. I found that during my career I always knew when it was time to leave one stage of my life behind and move to the next one. For example, after working for Boeing's helicopter flight controls group for seven years, I had become the electronics guru within that division. I was then promoted to supervise the avionics group, which was an area I was unfamiliar with. At first I was very hesitant to abandon my expertise and company status, but over time I regained that status several times over by establishing additional expertise. Each time there was always some risk involved with the process, but with proper planning, self-confidence, commitment, and a lot of hard work, the stages seemed to blend together nicely. Initially it was always a little unsettling because of the unknowns, but after doing it successfully several times, I realized the new challenges eventually became standard operating procedure and things soon fell into place until it was time for another stage.

Although change is difficult because of the uncertainty of the unknown, it is also freeing because it allows us to leave our mistakes behind. When we look back at our lives and remember the many events that seemed like insurmountable mountains at the time, we realize how our fear of the unknown was the real problem, and the obstacles that seemed so huge have just become distant memories. They may have altered our lives at the time, but they are now only parts of our past. Although it may not seem like it at the time, change is always for the better, as it offers us an opportunity to grow, but it is just that, an opportunity. If we fight change and stubbornly cling to our old ways, then not only will things not improve, they will get worse, as nothing stays the same.

INFLUENCE OTHERS

Thoughts influence other minds. Not only can strong minds influence material objects, but they can cause less-focused minds to follow them. Thoughts work to overcome the resistance of other minds even if their doctrines are false. Unethical religious and political leaders have used this to their advantage for years. If enough people believe something, then others will follow their line of reasoning, even if it is irrational. Rational thought and the will to pursue truth eventually overcome false opinions, but it can take a long time and a lot of suffering. The stronger and more focused irrational minds might triumph in the short run, but reason and truth will eventually win out.

Great leaders have succeeded in aligning their organizations by getting everyone's mind focused on pursuing a common goal. The power of a highly focused group is incredible. Leaders from Alexander the Great to George Washington were able to get the minds of their supporters aligned in such a way that their will was greater than the opposition. We see it all the time in sports, where seemingly less talented teams are able to beat teams with greater skill but far less focus. The reason that the great coaches are so successful is that they can focus the players toward a single purpose. There are many good examples in industry as well. So many really good companies lose direction when the founder or driving personality is no longer at the helm. Apple Inc. is a great example. Steve Jobs built the company, when he left it floundered, and when he returned Apple returned to greatness once again. It is not just the leaders' ideas that are important, but their ability to focus the minds of others. The commitment and confidence of the entire organization is what causes its prosperity. Companies that have no long-term selfless goals and only want to make money will soon perish as the winds of change will slowly tear them apart.

RATIONAL THOUGHT

Discrimination

Rational thought is the strongest tool we possess in our search for truth and happiness, but as a society we have gotten in the habit of delegating that capability to others. We have developed a cultural attitude of dependence on others for both our livelihoods and, unfortunately, our beliefs.

We live in a society that is divided into specialties. Our food is grown or raised by specialty farms, distributed by specialty transports, and sold in specialty markets. The same process is used for the creation of our clothes, the building of homes, all forms of transportation, and virtually everything else in life, including selecting specialties for our employment and hobbies. Depending on others for our physical needs is a practical expediency that allows us to create a complicated society, and there is nothing wrong with it; but our dependency goes further than that.

We expect the government to protect us, we expect our employers to take care of our medical and financial needs, and we expect schools and colleges to teach us truth; but our dependency has come with a price, because in return for their efforts, we have allowed them to think for us. We do this out of fear or laziness or self-interest, but whatever the reason, the result is a distorted view of reality. We do not realize the harm that they are causing, so we just go along. But we are what we think, and when we let others think for us we become less. The onus is on us to be discriminating consumers of information and be assured that what we are being told makes sense.

When we don't fully grasp the impact of our belief systems, we allow ourselves to judge others and justify our selfish behavior by being part of the crowd. We think that we are better than others because we share views with people we believe to be superior to us in some way; but time and time again we find these superior people to be disingenuous and hypocritical. Politics and religion are two of the main culprits, and both offer views that shape our lives. When our views are false, we make bad choices, resulting in difficult circumstances with which we are forced to deal. By letting others make decisions for us, we make our lives much more difficult.

Cultivation of the mind requires that we stay in the here and now. Our life plans lead us to experiences that require focus and careful thought. New situations continually arise, and we need to be ready and willing to deal with them. One way to avoid dealing with our life plans is to live in the past or future. If times are difficult, we might regret our past decisions or daydream about a future time when life is easier. If we are fearful, it is always the future that we fear, which can lead to paralysis of thought and action. However, if we can focus on the present and deal with whatever comes our way in a timely, honest, and direct manner, then we will surely be living our life plans to the fullest. Flights of fancy allow our minds to wander aimlessly. Directed thought, attention to details and pursuit of truth will enhance our lives and spiritual growth. Remember, we are never given anything that we cannot handle, and our greatest lessons are learned when things look the darkest.

Thoughts need to be focused and controlled to be discriminating. We are blessed with the ability to reason, but we do not always use it as well as we should. An undisciplined mind does great harm, but a disciplined mind does great good. Discrimination of fact from fancy is man's best educational tool, as truth comes from within. If information does not feel right, then it is probably an opinion looking for a victim.

Faith versus Blind Faith

Faith and hope are appropriate to get our journeys started, but we need caution, as they can become a slippery slope that leads to blind faith and conformity. There is nothing wrong with faith and hope as long as we realize they are just that. We have faith in our teachers, our health, our economy, and virtually everything else with which we deal, but it is not usually blind faith. For example, we have faith that our health will be good when we eat well, exercise moderately, and visit the doctor regularly. We have done what we think is practical and rational in order to take the necessary precautions, but after that we realize that things could go wrong; however, we use faith and hope to allow ourselves to stop worrying about them. It is simply a practical way to live our lives.

Blind faith is different. We have blind faith in our health when we over- or under eat, don't exercise, smoke or drink excessively, and never get medical advice. We hope that things will be OK, but no reasonable person could expect us to remain healthy long. In this case blind faith is a problem because we did not use our reason, good judgment, and effort to make the best decisions possible. In this example there is plenty of information available to make better decisions, but we chose not to use it. Many of us find numerous examples in our daily lives in which blind faith is the controlling factor. This is usually because we are afraid of facing the consequences of our situations. Clearly our best approach is to draw a line in the sand and start dealing with the truth of the situation ASAP. We need to let the past go and realize that what we have done and believed up to now is history. Today is the first day of the rest of our lives, and we need to start acting rationally. Our problems are simply lessons in life, and we need to deal with them.

What makes blind faith so bad is that we stop using our greatest gift, reason, and instead give in to fear. Once we do this, we open ourselves up to irrational beliefs. We will never find truth if we have no rational foundation for our thoughts. Searching for truth requires endless effort and discrimination. There are obstacles in our way, but we have the tools to navigate around them if only we are willing to use them.

Thoughts are Freeing

We are eternal beings fully capable of understanding and recognizing truth. Our worldviews are incredibly important to our spiritual growth. We need the self-confidence to take control of our minds and accept the responsibility for our lives. We must break away from the dependency of blindly accepting others' opinions, no matter whose they are.

A good start would be to write down our fundamental beliefs on a piece of paper. We should focus on the really key beliefs that guide our lives; the principles on which we base our decisions. Then ask should ourselves the following questions:

1. Why do I believe this?

2. Do I believe this because I have thought it all out and it makes the most sense to me?

3. Do I believe it because I am afraid not to?

4. Do I believe it because someone else told me it was true?

5. Do I even know what I believe?

If we have thought it all through and our present conclusion is the best one we can come up with, then we are headed in the right direction. Whether we are right or wrong is secondary. At least we are taking responsibility for our own thoughts. Truth will come to all of us in time, as long as we are searching for it. If we are still letting others tell us what to believe, then we will need to come to grips with our submission before we can become our own masters. Remember, we are minds and nothing else, so our ideas are who we are. We can ill afford to be less than what we can be. If our fears allow others to do our thinking for us, then our spiritual growth will remain stagnant. It is bad enough that we spend our lives fooling others, but it is inexcusable to fool ourselves. Integrity starts with our own beliefs.

We can live in slavery or under despotism, but if we think for ourselves, then we are free men and women living under difficult circumstances. But if we blindly follow the opinions of others, then we are slaves no matter what our stations in life might be. It is only when we put aside the veil of fear and hypocrisy and allow our rational minds to control our thoughts that we will start our steep ascent toward wisdom. Beginning the self-improvement process requires faith that it is possible as well as hope that we will succeed, but we will soon discard both as unnecessary when self-confidence and courage push them aside.

FALSE THOUGHTS

Our beliefs make us who we are so, if our beliefs are not true then we are less than we could be. What we think and why we think it are the essence of our nature. Just misunderstanding something is not an issue, because we are here to learn. The problem arises when we dedicate our entire lives to an idea or philosophy that our subconscious minds know is false. Whenever we ignore our subconscious, we usually regret it, but when we live lives out of sync with our subconscious minds, it causes a serious discord within us. It can cause debilitating physical and mental disabilities, stress, and irrational fears; misery follows self-deception. Our subconscious minds are continually trying to execute our life plans, and when we are living lies, that is not possible. No one builds a life plan based on false ideas.

Usually our fears drive us to false doctrines that lead us astray. We initially find comfort in conforming to the enthusiasm of others, and a weight seems to be lifted off our shoulders. The comfort of others can be very seductive; but over time, when we have digested the beliefs and they do not ring true, we begin to question what we are being told. We may be too afraid to voice our opinions, but we harbor the doubts inside us. If the philosophy is political or work related, we may fear the reaction of others, but if it is religious, we might even fear God's wrath. Whatever it is, we repress the feeling until we either burst out in full rejection of the doctrine or we bury it inside. It is the latter that eventually eats away at our health and self-respect. The sooner we weed out our false opinions, the sooner we will align ourselves with the cosmos and our planned paths.

The onus is on us to pursue truth, but all too often we take the easy road of least resistance. Religious beliefs are especially difficult to deal with because we had originally turned to them to help us with our self-doubts and fears. Now we realize that they did not bring us the answers that they promised, but we are committed to a lifestyle we are afraid to abandon. We need the self-confidence to look at our beliefs logically and discard those we cannot understand or know are wrong. When we need a leap of faith to build the foundations of our belief systems, then we can be assured our houses are built of cards.

ENLIGHTENMENT

What is enlightenment? Both Eastern and Western religious mystics speak of enlightenment, which is proclaimed to be the ultimate state of spiritual knowledge. Many religious zealots strive for this state of mind in hopes of breaking the karmic cycle of life and death. They often forgo all earthly comforts and adhere to a code of silence or austerity in hope of reaching an enlightened state. But how do we know if and when we become enlightened? Does the sky open up, or is there a spiritual experience that accompanies it? Do we all of a sudden commune with God, or do we die and go off to nirvana?

The process of enlightenment is the slow task of casting off our worldly illusions. It is the tedious process of unfolding our consciousness like the budding lotus blossom. One does not all of a sudden change from unenlightened to enlightened; it is not a eureka moment. Becoming enlightened is simply making progress in our search for truth. We live in a world of opinions that are represented to us as truths. The more prestigious an individual or organization, the more likely we are to accept their opinions. Organizations of all sizes and shapes try to impress us with their grandeur, opulence, and reputations in hopes of putting their opinions above reproach. But inevitably their doctrines do not prove true.

We are not ready for most of the world's truths. We would not understand them, because we have not built the proper foundation to grasp their significance. Truth has its own language, which we cannot fully grasp until we learn the words and the grammar. We need to learn the language of truth before we can begin to understand its subtleties; but when we finally do, truth will make innate sense. When we are ready for some aspect of truth, we will recognize it because it will feel right; it will fit into place like a puzzle piece. If we are still questioning a belief, then either we are not ready for it or it is not truth. Enlightenment is a path to understanding; a process without end.

FREE WILL

Although the Universal Consciousness controls the cosmos and causes it to constantly change, its future is not predestined. Each realm is like an eternal unscripted play that is continuously being written in real time. The play's evolution is determined by the combined decisions of each conscious unit. The wisdom of the Universal Consciousness is such that it has a good idea what each spirit will do at any point in time, but because they are all unique and have free will and independent minds, the outcome is not a certainty.

The world of ESP is full of accounts of people predicting the future. Although some events have come true with amazing accuracy, such as Edgar Cayce's prediction of finding the Nag Hammadi scrolls several years before they were discovered, many more have not. The problem with predicting the future is that free will exists, and as such there is no way to be 100 percent sure what is going to occur. Our future is probabilistic, not predetermined. Clearly there are those with the ability to look into the future, but what they are seeing is the possibility of what will come about, not what must come about. If people do not make the expected decisions, different outcomes will occur at both the personal and macro levels. It is never too late to change an event if it has not occurred. If life were predetermined, what a boring future we would have.

CONTEMPLATION AND MEDITATION

Learning to use the power of our minds requires mental discipline and concentration. Like any competency, the mind needs to be trained to function at a high level.

Meditation is focusing on nothing and requires openness, awareness, and expectation. Meditation is best for relaxing, and for attaining insight into our inner selves and the cosmos in general. Meditation is difficult because it requires shutting out all our thoughts. There are many books that offer advice on meditation techniques, but the Dalai Lama[46] offers as simple and straightforward a view as any I have seen. I paraphrase:

---

46 Dalai Lama, *The Universe in a Single Atom* page 158.

Sit in a comfortable position that requires no effort. Face a beige or nondescript wall with no sharp colors. Start out by making a silent pledge not to allow any thoughts to interfere with the session. Don't worry about the future or rue the past; just be aware of the present. This is vital, as we live in the past and future much of the time. One should allow thoughts to arise but let them flow away, never judging or even commenting on them. Eventually one gets a glimpse of mere absence of thought. No content is present, as it is just a state of awareness. This will start out as only short glimpses, but with practice and training these moments will last longer and longer. Eventually we will be able to grasp the experience of consciousness.

Once we learn to clear away our thoughts and completely empty our minds of sensory data, then we will have access to the spiritual world and its knowledge, as our minds never leave the spiritual world, they are just so cluttered with sensory data that we cannot access it. The ultimate mind control is meditation, which is a good way to clear our minds and focus our thoughts.

Contemplation is concentrating our thoughts on an object or a concept in such a way that we are completely focused on it. Contemplation is used with concepts to attempt to fully understand them or with objects to control them. Visualization is a useful aid to contemplation. We can envision how we want things to happen and focus our thoughts on the desired outcome, but if we have any doubts they will surely disrupt the outcome. A golf swing is a good example of this. We need to visualize the ball's flight, believe that it will happen, and then swing. If any other thought creeps into our minds during the process, the shot will never work. Contemplation is most successful when used by someone with a strong will and is best for changing our lives or making things happen.

Both meditation and contemplation are excellent ways to help strengthen and increase our mental capabilities.

AKASHIC RECORDS

I would like to take a short excursion to discuss a topic that readers may have run across and puzzled over during their searches. Some psychics, hypnotic regressionists, and religions maintain that there is a complete record of every idea that was ever thought throughout the history of mankind, which is known as the akashic records. They supposedly reside in the spiritual realm and are in the form of a giant tapestry. Each one of us has our own thread, which tells the story of our spiritual growth. Each line starts out dark because of our ignorance but slowly gets brighter as we pursue the path toward wisdom.

Supposedly there is a written record of every thought that we ever had, and by definition we are the ones that write that record. Theoretically these records are available to us in this life if we can properly focus our minds on them, because each person's record is also recorded in their subconscious. Nothing is hidden from us when we are ready and able to deal with it. Edgar Cayce was supposedly able to read the akashic records of others, from which he made some incredible predictions, many of which have come true. The records detail the true intent of each of our actions because they are a record of our thoughts, not just a visual record of our activities. It records not only our experiences but also the karma that goes with them. Reading and understanding the akashic records is difficult even if we attain access to them, because we see them through our own limited perspectives, as well as that of the psychic.

PHILOSOPHY

Philosophy is the search for truth. These days it is considered an esoteric subject pursued by only a few intelligentsia in limited scholastic circles. As a result of our focus on materialism and societal dependence, we live in a world where few people know what truth is or how to find it.

In fact, all too few of us are even interested in searching for it, as it pales in comparisons to our material pursuits; however, this has not always been the case. Twenty-five hundred years ago, the great cultures of the world put the search for truth at the forefront of importance. Between 1000 and 500 BC the Greek scholars were setting the stage for the great philosophers, Confucius created the Analects, the great Hindu leaders wrote the Upanishads, Buddha set forth the principles that later became known as the Dhammapada, and many of the great Hebrew prophets flourished. The ancient Greek philosophers were good examples of reason in search of life's answers. They may or may not have found truth, but they were rarely fooled by false doctrines. Ideas have their time, and those were the times when philosophy became of paramount interest across the globe. Fortunately many of these ideas have been recorded for all to read, and a great deal of truth can be gleaned from these works.

From a worldview perspective, philosophy has an advantage over science because it allows us to go beyond the natural realm and see the spiritual force behind it. Science postulates reality in the cosmos, but it limits our understanding of what might have created the cosmos and why. Philosophy allows us to more fully understand and evaluate the multitude of scientific analyses that we are inundated with, while at the same time weighing the contribution of thousands of years of religious thought, without buying into the various creeds. It is like the difference between an operators' manual and a design manual. Science is working on the operators' manual, studying how things work, and philosophy is working on the design manual, studying why things work. Both are important, but each one has its own special perspective.

Developing a worldview is a philosophical exercise in thought. We cannot hope to understand ourselves until we understand the world around us. We need to see the world as it really is and understand its purpose in order to best take advantage of all it offers us. We need to let philosophy back into our lives, as it is the true science of the mind.

JOURNEY OF THOUGHT

Thoughts control material objects, and they control the world around us, but most importantly, they control our future. We become what we think. Thoughts are real, everlasting, all-powerful, and transcendent, and they are ours for eternity. Our thoughts energize and influence whatever we come in contact with.

When we allow others to think for us, we are abandoning our greatest gift. Without the courage to stand behind our beliefs, life wears away at our spirits. We do not need to live stressful and fearful lives, but we bring them on by our false hopes and illogical perspectives. It is crucial to be true to ourselves, because personal integrity is a requirement for a life of virtue and contentment. We all have the capability to understand the truth, which will eventually free us from the karmic cycle of the natural realm. The sooner we stop following others, the sooner we will free ourselves from the bonds of the cosmos.

Over time we will attain incredible capabilities, but even at this stage our minds have the power to change our world if we can learn to harness and enhance them through concentration, commitment, and rational thought. Enthusiasm is a powerful means of amplifying our thoughts, and when coupled with self-confidence, persistence, and focus we will surely change our world and ourselves for the better.

Our journey is one of thought, not travel. We go places and learn different things while on this earth, but the task of perfecting the soul is improving our minds. What is changing within us is not our capability to obtain material accomplishments, but our spiritual state. All the changes that we will ever experience will take place within our minds.

CHAPTER 8

SPIRITUALITY

The things men count great are nothing to us.
The things we seek are not of the flesh
but are only the perfected state of the Soul.
When ye as men learn that nothing but
progress of Soul can count in the end,
then truly ye are free from all bondage,
free to work in the harmony of Law.

– The Emerald Tablets

Key Concept: *Living a spiritual life is following*
     our life plans.

WHAT IS SPIRITUALITY?

Being spiritual is the process of following and executing our life plans.

Spirituality is a commonly misunderstood concept and is usually confused with religion, praying or the ascetic life. In fact, this could not be farther from the truth as it has nothing to do with creeds or beliefs. Spirituality is diligently attending to life's day-to-day problems, which allows us to get the most out of those experiences. We are on this earth

143

for the sole purpose of strengthening and growing our spirit so it helps to understand what that entails. Our life plan addresses our most pressing spiritual deficiencies, which are the key elements that we need to enhance in order to optimize our near-term growth. In order to know what aspects of our spiritual nature we should strengthen, it helps to have a better understanding of what attributes our spiritual nature consists and their impact on our lives. In the paragraphs below we will review the six primary attributes and some of the key characteristics of our spirit. By evaluating our strengths and weaknesses against our spiritual attributes and characteristics we can see where we need to concentrate our efforts in order to live happier and more productive lives.

KEY ATTRIBUTES OF THE SPIRIT

The following six attributes are distinct yet work together as a system such that we hardly recognize their individual existence. Strengthening these attributes will help us get the most out of our life plan.

1. Desire and Aspiration

Desire is what makes us want to obtain something, embrace change, and act. It is the need that we all have that makes us execute our life plans. Without desire we would be stuck in an eternal state of boredom and complacency. We would never do anything, go anywhere, or learn anything. Desire is the initial cause of everything that ever was or ever will be; however, there is a negative effect of desire when it focuses on the material world. Desire causes all the problems in this world, as we can desire to follow a path that is counterproductive to our growth. The material world holds many attractions for the immature spirit that can lead us astray. Chasing selfish rewards leads to negative consequences and misery. It is imperative that we learn which desires lead to contentment and which lead to misfortune and hardship.

Buried within our psyches is our aspiration to perfect our spirits. When we are spiritually young, our material desires overcome our spiritual aspirations, but eventually the allure of materialism fades and we realize that we can become no more than what we aspire to be. The Universal Consciousness aspires to perfect itself, and because we have a self within us, in time we learn to aspire to the same end. It is worth reflecting on the difference between desire and aspiration. Desire encourages us to obtain, whereas aspiration encourages us to become. Aspiration is the critical ingredient within our nature that allows us to keep going no matter how difficult it is. Aspiration gives us the impetus to perfect our souls.

2. Will

Our wills give us the determination to follow through on our desires and aspirations. Simply having a desire is not enough; we need the commitment to make it happen. Our life plans are filled with obstacles with which we need to deal. They require both the desire to deal with our circumstances and the capacity to see that desire through. Giving up in the middle of one of life's lessons only results in another lesson some time later. Our wills give us the strength to execute our lessons.

Will is the power behind mind over matter because it focuses and amplifies our thoughts. The Universal Consciousness's thoughts imagined the cosmos, but it was its will that allowed the cosmos to be created, and it is its will that sustains it. Everything that exists has been created through the power of ideas, but it is the will behind those ideas that is the force that allows the ideas to come into existence and be sustained. It is the Universal Consciousness's will that controls the matter in the universe, and it is our wills that allow us to modify and fine-tune the small part of the universe in which we live.

Willpower is synonymous with self-control, as it allows us to manage our lives. Life is a continual series of temptations and challenges.

Our life plans present us with various options at every turn; we need to discriminate between our many choices and select the right path. Taking what appears to be the easy road and pursuing short-term gratification inevitably leads us astray. Our willpower keeps us from being seduced by the enticements of the roadblocks that exist in the material world. The stronger our wills, the better chance we have of making and pursuing the right choices. The will to resist is as important as the will to pursue.

In many ways we are defined by our wills. Our wills are a big factor in determining how we approach life, and to a large extent, how successful we are. Knowing our wills are strong enough to accomplish our goals gives us the confidence to begin a new challenge and the determination to stay with it when times get difficult. That knowledge provides us the capability to act upon the choices that we make. The strength of a person's will determines if he or she is motivated or lazy, energetic or lethargic, a leader or a follower. Our wills determine the type of people that we are, our reliability, and how we go about our daily lives.

3. Reason

Our most valuable asset in following our spiritual plans and obtaining wisdom is our ability to reason. Reason requires the ability to be logical, understand concepts, form opinions, and draw conclusions. Reason allows us to evaluate experiences and make judgments as to the true nature of things. How well we reason and how often we use reason to make our decisions is an indication of our spiritual maturity. All too often we make decisions based on superficial information and then convince ourselves that we are acting out of reason when all we are really doing is rationalizing our behavior. Spiritual growth requires the enhancement of all of our reasoning skills in an effort to discover truth. We need to view all sides of an issue equally in order to appreciate the subtleties.

Discrimination is a key aspect of reason. In our world of illusion, discrimination is the most important power that we have. We are continually bombarded with false and deceptive information, and we need to learn how to find our way through the maze and toward the truth. Discrimination allows us to ignore the distractions and focus on what is important. We must continually question the motivation behind what we are being told and understand who will benefit from a resulting course of action. Ultimately we need to pay less attention to the source of the data and more attention to what is being said. When we get caught up in the grandeur of the source, we can confuse opinion with truth.

4. Emotions

Emotions are our feelings, which are the essence of who we are, and they can be positive or negative or somewhere in between. Positive emotions like happiness, love, contentment, and joy provide us great comfort. Negative emotions like sadness, grief, jealousy, panic, and fear can be very upsetting. Emotions are thoughts at heightened states of energy that affect our psyches in different and unique ways.

One of the main goals of a life plan is to teach us about emotions. Our experiences allow us to understand the many aspects of our feelings. We cannot know success if we have not experienced failure. Emotions control our lives, and we use them to evaluate if things are going well for us or not.

A key element of spiritual maturity is how well we control our emotions. Spiritual lessons are better learned when we are patient and keep even dispositions. When we lose our tempers, we lose our rationality and close our minds to alternative views.

Equilibrium is the key to our emotions. Emotions are on polar scales like happy/sad and love/hate. We must not get too high when things go our way, for life will surely balance out. Conversely, we should not get too low when things look their worst, as they too will turn around soon.

People like to say "don't sweat the small stuff." Well, don't sweat the big stuff either. Everything always works out in the end. Indeed, if we should measure ourselves at all, it should be against what makes us lose our tempers.

5. Imagination (Creativity)

Creativity is the ability to transcend traditional rules, ideas, patterns, and relationships in order to develop original concepts and approaches. Creativity is an inherent and a prized capability in all of us. Whenever we see something new or done differently, we note it and even enjoy bringing it to another person's attention. Museums, art galleries, plays, and musical performances are all tributes to man's creativity. It allows us to adapt to changes, solve problems, and work through our life experiences. We admire creativity because it is embedded within our nature.

What we seldom recognize is how much creativity was required to develop and evolve the complex world in which we live. We created our bodies, built the environment around us, and continually create the circumstances in which we exist by way of all the day-to-day decisions that we have to make. We depend on our creativity for our very existence.

Despite all our creative forces that we apply in our lives today, the future is where our real creativity will emerge. At this stage of development, most of our creativity is used to make slight modifications to existing ideas. Everything that exists on earth has a template that was created in the spiritual world. For example, although we are each unique and had a hand in creating our own body, the human form was already created, and what we did was to make minor adaptations to it for our own purposes. The earth and our environment already exist, and we make minor adaptations to it for our own needs. As such, our creativity is learning how to adapt existing concepts to our personal desires. A time will come when we will be capable of working with a clean slate. Our wisdom and understanding will be such that our imagination will be able to create things that have no template. The distant future holds untold opportunities for all of us.

6. Communication

The spiritual language is universal and innate to all beings. In the spiritual world, communication is common to all spirits and occurs instantly and at will. Here on earth, communication is one of our most challenging tasks, because we are forced to deal with it through our five physical senses. In the spiritual realm, communication is through thought, so there are no language barriers.

The barriers to communication in the spiritual world are caused by the different levels of understanding. It is difficult for us to communicate freely with very advanced beings, as our immature souls do not have an adequate understanding of many of the universal principles. This prevents souls from different levels from being able to fully communicate with each other. The younger spirits simply do not understand what they are being shown. Likewise, it would be difficult for us to communicate with spirits much lower than ourselves for the same reason.

We need to learn to use communication to inform, not control. Unfortunately much of our communication is used to badger, intimidate, and otherwise make ourselves appear better than others. We change other people's lives not by differing with them, but through example. Spiritual communication is not the conversion of others to a point of view, but offering others an awareness of new and different perspectives. Very often it is not so much what we say but how we say it that truly matters.

Maturity of Attributes

When we reach the level of maturity where we incarnate into a human form, we begin taking responsibility for our actions, and the process of karma begins. Table 2 below shows the normal state in which we begin and the goals for which we should strive. The end goal or final state that we will achieve is not available to us at this point and indeed may always be changing.

Attribute	Initial State	Goal	End State
Desire	Material Needs	Wisdom	?
Will	Impulsive	Self-Control	?
Reason	Opinionated	Logical	?
Emotion	Selfish	Impersonal Love	?
Communication	Confusing	Complete	?
Creativity	Imitative	Original	?

Maturity of Attributes
Table 2

PERSONALITY TRAITS OR THE CHARACTERISTICS OF THE SOUL

The various attributes of our souls blend together in different ways to create what we refer to as our personalities. Our characteristics define the boundaries in which we operate. The stronger our attributes, the better able we are to develop positive personality characteristics. These characteristics can either assist or impede our spiritual growth, depending on how we have cultivated them. It is in our best interests to strengthen and refine these characteristics, as they will help define us and allow us to get the most out of our experiences.

Personal Responsibility

Personal responsibility requires the aspiration to be all that we can be, the discrimination to know what is right, and the will to see it through. "*Theology teaches man to cast his burdens on others, but philosophy tells him to carry them himself.*"[47] God has tasked us with the personal responsibility for the growth of our own souls, and a mature spirit is one that has accepted that responsibility. We are who we are and where we are because of the decisions that we have made. Accepting the consequences of our decisions and learning from our mistakes is the whole point of life. Everyone has problems, which is why we are here. Hiding behind a facade of deceit and hypocrisy does not strengthen our spirits, but weakens them. We make decisions that have consequences, so we need to learn to live with those consequences openly and with integrity. It is always best to get our dirty laundry out in the open where we can deal with it. Facing our failures is difficult, but ignoring them is disastrous. Self-criticism should be the start of the analysis of any situation. If we don't take responsibility for our actions, then we are delegating that responsibility to others. This is especially true when we follow a creed or organization and let it dictate our views. As Manly P. Hall said and I paraphrase: *those who seek masters are rewarded by becoming slaves.* As we mature, we begin to realize that we are the cause of all our problems, and we are also the solution to them.

Self-Discipline

Self-discipline is the combination of desire and will. We almost always know what is best for us, but when our willpower is lacking we have a tendency to put our material desires ahead of our better judgment. The more wisdom we have, the more self-discipline we demonstrate. There is no worse feeling than being out of control, so if we cannot control ourselves, how can we expect to be happy? Take it to the extreme and think of the times that you have been completely out of control, such as standing on land shaking from an earthquake or in a car skidding on ice. Your first feeling is complete fear. Living a life in which

---

47 Manly P. Hall: Words to the Wise page 114

we feel out of control, even for short periods, makes spiritual growth much more difficult. Whether the problem is alcohol, food, drugs, relationships, or whatever, we need to take control of our lives, one piece at a time if necessary, by making the decisions that we know are in our best interests.

Goodness

Goodness is a complicated combination of desire, discrimination, will, and emotion. Desiring to do things for the betterment of others, while taking no personal credit, is truly a pillar of spirituality and goodness. We give our time and our wealth for a number of reasons. Unfortunately, all too many donors want the world to know how generous they are. If a person's name is on a monument, then it is highly unlikely that his gift actually strengthened his spirituality. On the other hand, anonymous gifts and backroom services will surely hold us in good stead.

Patience

Patience is a combination of our desires, will, and emotions. Patience is being strong, steadfast, and humble in the face of adversity and opportunity. First we need patience with ourselves, and then with others. The cosmos is in a continuous state of motion, and everything comes to those who are aware enough to know what they want and patient enough to wait for its arrival; every idea has its time. Trying to change the pace of nature, be it faster or slower, will cause nothing but despair. The better road is to wait for events to unfold and be compassionate for those that do not.

Decision Making

Reason, and in particular discrimination, is the key to decision making. The law of karma tells us that if we follow the path of wisdom and goodness, the rewards in this life and beyond will follow and our many lives on this earth will be happy and productive. But how do we know what action to take to best pursue our life plans? Actually, it is pretty straightforward. ***Do what you know is right but do not want to do.*** Our instincts best tell us the correct course of action. If we allow ourselves to act with integrity, then making the right decisions in life will be automatic. The more difficult the problem is, the more important the decision.

Self-deception, which has its roots in fear, is the worst thing we can do, because it is impossible to find truth when we are living a lie. Acknowledging our strengths and weaknesses allows us to understand where we are and what we need to work on and will also help us recognize our important life lessons when they arise.

The Tao[48] teaches us to surrender to the ways of the cosmos. Surrender does not mean capitulation, it means do not resist; go with the flow, and guide the situation in its natural course or way. The creative force of nature is constantly flowing around us, and we do not have the strength or wisdom to resist it. When making choices, we must listen to our inner selves and follow our gut feelings. Whenever we feel we should do something but don't, we inevitably regret it. Our subconscious minds have great knowledge, which we can tap into if we do not fight those inner thoughts. They are there to protect and assist us, so we need to use them. As we ride along in life's ebb and flow, we should try to ensure the world is a better place because we passed through it.

Self-Confidence

Self-confidence is a combination of reasoning, desire, will, and emotion. It is much easier to succeed if we are confident that we can do it. Mind controls matter, and a focused and determined mind can perform

---

48 Ancient Chinese philosophy of Lao-Tzu; the Tao is "the way."

many tasks that we might view as miracles. Knowing that we are gods in the making and that we are here to learn through our mistakes should help reduce our fears and allow us to take risks that we might otherwise shun. It is fear and self-doubt that create the illusion that others control our lives.

Attitude

Attitude is a combination of desire, reasoning, and emotion. Our attitudes determine how we approach our problems and how we handle our successes and failures. A positive, can-do attitude allows us to view the world and our problems in a favorable manner. Although our attitudes are simply accumulations of thought patterns, they have a huge impact on our lives. We are what we think, and negative thoughts attract negative circumstances.

We have a tendency to get down on life when things don't go our way, but we need to keep the bigger picture in mind; today's problems are a result of poor past decisions. The sooner that we burn off the old karma, the sooner we can get into more positive parts of our life plans, but if we handle our problems poorly, we can create even more karma. The fastest way to change our world is by changing our attitudes toward it. It is important to remain positive no matter how dire the circumstance appears. We must continually remind ourselves that we caused these situations by making mistakes somewhere in our past, and we added them to our life plans because we wanted to learn how to deal with them properly. The tides of fortune cannot afflict those that benefit from adversity as well as success.

A wise soul judges itself, not others, as it is our judgments that cause us pain. We have a tendency to not accept the weaknesses of others, and yet we do not acknowledge the same weaknesses in ourselves. Offering understanding and support instead of judgment and incrimination is the best path. No one in the spiritual world expects us to be perfect or anywhere near it, so we need not expect perfection from others either. All too often we judge others to divert attention from our own mistakes. Envy and jealousy are judgments; we would be better served by worrying about our own behavior. In the end, we will value our lives on how well our souls progressed, not on our material accomplishments.

Courage

Courage requires the reasoning to decide what is right, the integrity to do what is right, and the will to see it through. Personal courage in the face of adversity is a sure sign of a mature spirit. A good way of strengthening our spirits is to challenge opposing positions for the betterment of others, especially if it is at a personal cost. The proof of our courage is not that we conquer the world, but that the world does not conquer us.

Grace

Ultimately we need to acquire grace. Grace is accepting others for what they are, flaws and all, and realizing that like us, they are doing the best they can to learn the lessons of life. Our world is one challenge after another, but we need to understand that the nature of our problems is self-generated and remember our misfortune is merely a debt we owe to life, so we need to bear it gracefully.

Maturity of Personality Traits

Similar to the attributes, our personalities evolve from the initial state at which we enter humanity to much more mature states, as shown in Table 3.

Characteristic	Initial State	Goal	End State
Responsibility	Depends on Others	Leads	?
Self-Discipline	Chaotic Life	Controlled	?
Goodness	Self-Absorbed	Ethical	?
Patience	Contrary	Tolerant	?
Decision Making	Emotional	Logical/Thorough	?
Self-Confidence	Insecure	Self-Assured	?
Attitude	Blames Others	Positive	?
Courage	Fearful	Intrepid	?
Grace	Selfish	Kind	?

Personality Traits

Table 3

ASPECTS OF WISDOM

When our spirits begin to mature, we begin to see the world a little differently. Life becomes a little easier, and we view our world and those around us a bit more gently. Each unit of consciousness is disguised as some animate or inanimate object. Each entity is working at a level where it can best learn the lessons that are most important for its spiritual growth. There are many different levels or cycles of life. The ancient Emerald Tablets claim that there are twenty-four major levels, and humans are on level fifteen from the bottom. Swedenborg, the sixteenth-century mystic, tells us that each level has an almost infinite number of sublevels, almost as many levels as there are beings. Regardless of whether those numbers are accurate or not, we are all operating under and learning about the same truth. The following are a few aspects of wisdom that we become more attuned to as we mature.

Beauty

Beauty occurs when we get a glimpse of the divine. Nature appears beautiful to us because it is the reflection of the divine's nature. Perceiving beauty is the process of evoking a positive emotional response within us to an object or an idea. Beauty appears when there is harmony between the vibrations of the beautiful and our own vibrations. As such, beauty is not just in the perceived object, but is in us as well. The more developed our vibrations, the more beauty we perceive. The beauty that we see in others is a reflection of ourselves, and in time we will learn to appreciate the beauty that exists in all.

Love

As we progress along our journey, we come to have a better understanding of who we are and the nature and role of others who assist us along the way. Manly P. Hall says that love progresses from the personal to the impersonal. We are on an emotional ascent toward impersonal love and compassion for humanity and all living things. It is easy to love our families and friends, but loving all mankind is a lot more difficult. It is hard to appreciate people when they are acting selfishly. We spend most of our lives trying to outdo others in our pursuit of material gains, but we need to realize that the only person worth competing with is us. How well we are perfecting our own souls is the only metric of value. We need to appreciate that everyone we meet is going through the same struggles that we are, and no matter how poorly they act, we need to appreciate their value and contribution to our learning process.

Learning to love all of nature's creatures is part of the maturing process. Man is not the only being on this planet that needs our love. We live in a differentiated world, where everything appears to be separate. Everything that is alive is part of the Universal Consciousness; every animal, insect, plant, microbe, everything.

We are here to learn to love all of mankind, and mankind is here to learn to love us, but we cannot love others until we learn to love ourselves. Too many of us are always down on ourselves because we do not realize who we are. We compare our accomplishments to the material accomplishments of others, and we all too often feel that we come up short, but the spiritual world holds no stock in material accomplishments. We need to get to know ourselves better and appreciate that we are key elements within the Universal Consciousness. We may be immature, but we will eventually blossom into fully mature divine members of this august entity. Our future is to be a spiritual being working in coordination with the infinite number of other beings. We are each a god in the making, and we need to treat ourselves accordingly and learn how to handle the powerful energies of love more responsibly.

If we had to make a choice to love our fellow man or love God, God would surely prefer that we love our fellow man, because in doing so we would love God as well.

Balance

A key aspect in our spiritual ascent to perfection is balance. Each of us has developed certain aspects of his or her spiritual nature to a higher level than others. Eventually we need to bring everything into balance, and we do that by working on our weaknesses. Mozart was reputed to be a good example of a spirit that reached the peak of one aspect of his consciousness while leaving other aspects less developed. Most of us are less likely to hone a particular aspect of our nature to such an extent without bringing the other elements along as well. But it is our journey, we can do it any way we please, and the law of karma will show us the wisdom of our choices. The goal of life is to align our spirits with that of the Universal Consciousness. This takes time and effort, but all souls eventually succeed. To live a spiritual life is to strengthen one or more of our spiritual attributes, which in turn will strengthen our spiritual characteristics. Following our life plans is the most efficient and reliable way to do this.

Temperance goes hand in hand with balance. Everything that we do must be done in moderation; too much of anything besides wisdom, understanding, and love is a problem. We become unbalanced when we focus our efforts so heavily in a single area that we lose perspective on how it and we fit into the whole. Letting our desires become obsessions biases our lessons such that we do not fully appreciate the circumstances with which we need to deal. For example, everyone simultaneously wears multiple hats in life, like being a parent, sibling, friend, child, employee, employer, teammate, etc. Totally focusing on work or sports or a hobby or any single responsibility to the exclusion of the others should be avoided. Selecting particular areas of focus and following particular paths of interest are fine as long as we recognize them for what they are and do not ignore other aspects of our lives. The truly wise have developed great temperance.

UNDERSTANDING

Understanding comes from the complex integration of wisdom and emotion and is a higher level of consciousness than either one. *Wisdom comes from realizing the highest emotional truths, and understanding comes from feeling the highest wisdom.* Wisdom allows us to feel *for* others (pity, sympathy) while understanding allows us the empathy to feel *with* them. We know what they are feeling because we have been there ourselves. Understanding is so difficult because it requires appreciating all the emotional responses that accompany each circumstance. We are unable to achieve understanding until we fully grasp the nuances behind each issue. It takes a long time to attain the experiences that are needed, but once we are able to realize enough truth and feel the accompanying emotions, then a whole new world of consciousness will open up for us. It is understanding that will allow us to become mature spirits ready to take our rightful places within the Universal Consciousness; understanding is the key to freedom within the spiritual realms.

AFFLICTIONS OF THE SOUL

Mankind suffers from a few common afflictions that impede our progress. It is to our advantage to evaluate ourselves to see how we might lessen our dependence on them.

Egotism

Self-exaltation condemns us to future karma. We need to set aside our self-centered perspectives and realize that we are all part of the single entity that I call the Universal Consciousness. Our fixation on putting ourselves above others stunts our spiritual growth and locks us into many difficult lives. Our only hope to lighten our karmic load is to think of the universal good, not our personal advantage, before making decisions. The following afflictions are identified with egotism: pride, greed, anger, envy, craving, spite, deceit, meanness, cruelty, and resentment, to name only a few. If we as a civilization could ever rid ourselves of these feelings, our growth would be enormous.

Materialism

Our materially oriented society has come with a huge psychological burden that we need to understand and deal with. Science and technology have made great progress in giving us creature comforts and medicine and explaining various aspects of nature, so it is hard for most of us to criticize them, let alone consider giving them up. Nearly everywhere we look, the material world seems to be providing us newfound comforts. However, we are consumed by the desire to amass great wealth, prestige, and comforts. This fixation has caused us to focus our desires on things that are unimportant in the spiritual realm. Our efforts are devoted to satisfying our sensual desires while we ignore our intellectual and emotional needs. We value cars, gemstones, and big houses above knowledge, friendship, and service to others. Yet we get no long-term satisfaction out of our possessions, which are often used to make us appear better than others and are then discarded. The world is mental and we are minds. Ideas are our products, and every thought, every idea, every emotion is there for us to draw on forever. The only material objects that are important are those that help us learn our lessons. When the lesson is over, their value is gone.

We need to become detached from the rewards of our labor. Detachment means placing the proper value on the material rewards and honorariums that we receive for our many efforts. Instead of focusing on our compensation, we need to focus on how well we deal with our experiences. We need jobs so that we can earn money to live, so getting paid well enough to take care of our families' needs is essential. People should be appropriately compensated for their efforts. The problem arises when we get greedy. For example, a corporate executive should worry more about how well he or she is taking care of the company than how well he or she is being compensated. Sports figures and other entertainers should worry about how well they perform, not how much they earn. Wealth gained through proper industrious effort is a suitable reward and should be welcomed, but wealth gained through dishonest activities is an abomination. Detachment is properly valuing those rewards.

Downplaying the importance of materialism is not saying we should discard our every possession and join the ascetic life, as Buddha explained the folly of severe depravation. Asceticism is not the answer to breaking the karmic cycle. We are far better off living modest lives of selfless service to others, ethical behavior in all things, and the pursuit of true understanding of ourselves and others, than trying to cut the karmic cycle short. We will not suffer if we do not cause others to suffer. If we want peace in our lives, we ought to remember the ancient wisdom:

> *Only possess the material things that we need to live a simple life, as no one will desire to steal them. Keep a low profile and no one will care what we do. Do not try to be better than our fellow man and no one will compete with us.*

In truth, we inwardly seek freedom from materialism yet we chase it every day. Peace of mind and happiness are the sacrifices that we make as a result of our material fixations. We need to develop a new perspective on materialism and the torment that it brings with it. Pressure in life comes from within and is the result of how we react to external stimuli. If we do not let life bother us, then we will not feel its stress. Our self-imposed expectations for both ourselves and others cause our problems as we create unrealistic standards of measurement. We need to have realistic expectations for ourselves and no expectations for others. No one takes his or her material possessions and accolades into the spiritual world. We need to focus on becoming, not acquiring, for we exist on the level of our thoughts, not our possessions.

PRAYER

If there is any one thing that we connect with spirituality, it is prayer. Prayer is communication with a deity. Prayer comes in one of three versions: (1) we praise God, (2) we petition him for benefits or assistance, and (3) we listen to him. Prayer is a powerful force, but it does not work the way most people think it does.

We love to praise God and thank him for all our blessings, but God is not interested in our praise or thanks. Long ago he rose above the human characteristics of vanity and jealousy. He wants our love, not our glorification. He wants our efforts, not our adoration. It does not do any harm to idolize God, but it should not be used as a substitute for right actions.

We might feel better about ourselves and our situations after praising God, but he expects more from us than praise.

When we have problems that seem too difficult for us to deal with, it is common for us to ask God to take our burdens from us. The reasoning often goes that if we praise him enough, then in return he will do us a favor. But asking for help is not going to convince him to solve our problems; he gave us our problems so that we could learn lessons that we need. He is not going to eliminate our burdens, because we need these experiences to grow; besides, God already learned these lessons, and it is now time for us to learn them. He has given us the sole responsibility to perfect our souls, and he has provided us all the necessary tools, guidance, and assistance to do so. In fact, the whole concept of convincing God to change his plan is unrealistic. Not only does he already know our every thought, but he knows our every need and provides for it well in advance. By the time the problem gets to us, all we need to do is deal with it. Trying to give our problems back to God will not work.

This is not to say that prayer does not have great value but the real value in prayer is twofold:

1. Prayer allows us to organize our thoughts and focus on what is really important to us. It is a quiet time that we can use to talk to our spirit guides, maybe get their feedback as to how we should proceed, or just unburden ourselves with things we do not want to share with others; a cleansing of our frustrations.

2. Most importantly, prayer works because our minds are powerful enough to influence both matter and other people's thoughts. In other words, we can help cause our prayers to come true without divine intervention.

There have been numerous studies done that showed prayer to be an effective tool in improving someone's recovery on a statistical basis. It made no difference if those praying had a religious affiliation or were from a secular group; the outcome was the same. Concentrated thought and prayer are excellent ways to change our health or someone else's. Group prayer is a good example of the power of multiple minds focusing on a single goal. Thought controls matter and influences mind, and the stronger the thought, the stronger the influence. If we could pull together as a nation, or better yet, a world, and pray or somehow continually focus our attention on specific issues, they would be readily resolved. Someday mankind will be able to accomplish this with regularity, but not yet.

ACHIEVING OUR LIFE PLANS

The Goal

If the goal of the spirit is perfection, then spirituality must be living a life that leads us toward the goal. The underlying criterion for growth is the requirement to put forth effort. There are no shortcuts to perfect the soul. Belief does not get it done, and no one will bestow it on us. Effort does not mean pain or suffering, nor does it even mean unpleasantness. It means that we need to pursue the ideal of perfection, because if we are not open to it, then it will not find us. We need to take it upon ourselves to maximize the precious time that we have here on earth to learn our lessons as well as we can.

We do not need to give up the desire for pleasure. We just need to realize that the only true and lasting pleasure is the pursuit of wisdom, understanding, and love. When we realize that appeasing our egos is not satisfying our souls and we yearn for a more rewarding pursuit, then we will have made a huge step forward.

Stay in the Present

We need to train ourselves to stay focused on the life and problems with which we are presently dealing. When we think about the future and all the unknowns, we allow fear to slip into our lives. We worry about things that are out of our control. There is nothing wrong with planning for the future, but when worry sets in we have crossed the line. For example, we can prepare for a future job by getting educated now. Researching what career we want to pursue and pursuing the training we will need is healthy; worrying about being able to find a job after we are trained is not.

Ruing past decisions or basking in our previous successes is not productive either; what is done is in the past, and there is no such thing as going back. We occasionally think how nice it would be to return to a simpler time that we really enjoyed. Maybe it was a place that we lived in our childhood, or an earlier home where we had so much fun. Then we go there and realize that it has all changed. The buildings and landscape are all different; most of the people that we knew are gone or have changed. We are strangers in a place where we were once accepted as family. It just is not the same, and we know it never will be. Even by trying to go back, we find ourselves moving forward. We are swept along by the tides of time. The answer is to make the life that we are living today just as wonderful as our memory of times gone by. Do not wish for the old; commit to the new.

We need to *forgive and forget*. Life would be easier for all if we were not troubled by other minds and did not let our minds trouble others. We get drawn out of the present when we fume over injustices of the past or fear the future. If the Universal Consciousness believes in forgetting our mistakes when we learn our lessons, then we should also. We need to learn to let go of the past and start new each day.

Appreciate what is Important

Stop Worrying

We need to keep our challenges in perspective. If we deal with the small details in a timely manner, the big stuff will take care of itself.

Realistically we cannot totally stop worrying about life, but we do not need to let it consume us either. We signed up to deal with these problems, and the point of the experience is to learn a lesson, no matter how difficult it may appear. It is worth remembering that no one has ever had more on his plate than he can handle. When things look the bleakest and all appears lost, sit down, relax, and try to see the humor in it all. We should remind ourselves, "Only I could have gotten myself into this big a mess, and only I can get myself out of it." Sleep on it, chuckle over it, but then deal with it. It won't be long before we miraculously find our way through the maze. We do not need to know where the path will lead, only where to place our feet for the next step.

Why

Why we do something is the only thing of importance in understanding and evaluating our motivation. Journalists learn that there are seven questions they need to ask in order to get their story: who, what, where, when, why, how, and how much. That may be fine for a newspaper story, but when it comes to understanding and evaluating ourselves, the only question of importance is *why*. We are the only ones that understand our fears, needs, and aspirations. As such, we are the only ones capable of judging our own actions. The spiritual world understands our whys, but it is far too wise to judge us. Only we are capable of understanding our thoughts and acting accordingly. It is not what we do, but why we do it that counts.

Respect Life

Life is a precious resource. Many spirits want to incarnate, but we were given the opportunity to live our lives because we were judged to be the most fit to learn the lessons available. Suicide, murder, and abortion are selfish and unjustifiable acts because they waste precious resources. Taking a life to avoid misfortune or responsibility is morally corrupt. It is only acceptable when it advances the good of others; for example, a soldier defending his country or a martyr defending his cause. When we have learned everything that we can in this life, we will die the death that was meant for us. Taking our lives or another's deprives the Universal Consciousness of an opportunity to teach its lessons. Life is a valuable commodity that should never be wasted.

Self-Reliance

Reason and discrimination refuse the comforts of conformity. We are under continual pressure to agree with our peers. It is easier to seek the companionship of those that agree with us than to follow the path of independent and contrary ideas, which is often the path to truth. We need our thoughts challenged and our positions evaluated in order to refine our understanding. Conformity is complying with the views of those that we associate with, but not necessarily the majority view. Conformity leads to misguided beliefs and holier-than-thou attitudes that unfairly judge others. Nationalism, religion, race, and politics are ripe for becoming passionate and destructive values that tear at our spirits. Our society is filled with opinions that are rarely right but widely held. If we constantly seek the approval of others for our opinions, we will forfeit our sense of rationality and discrimination, and in the process we will diminish our spiritual growth. We need strong individuality and a commitment to the pursuit of truth. Finding truth is not so much dispensing with the trivia of material things as much as it is dispensing with the trivia of our precious notions.

The world is constantly changing, and we change with it, so our viewpoints should change as well. Getting mired in a particular train of thought keeps us from fully experiencing our life plans. When we learn something new, we can only benefit from it when we allow it to change our minds.

Difficult Lessons

Some lessons seem overbearing when we first come upon them, and it helps to establish a plan on how to move forward. This gives us a sense of control and helps put boundaries around the problem. Issues like disease, a challenging relationship, or any other serious hardship need to be dealt with rationally.

1. We should take responsibility for the issue. We caused it so we can learn from it.

2. We need to align ourselves with it. We should bless it and all those involved because they are assisting us in the process.

3. We should surrender to it. We need to feel it and accept it and be positive about it. There is nothing wrong with accepting the illusions of life, but we must not be captured by them. Dealing with difficult lessons is part of our growth process, but then we must move on.

4. We should deal with the problem openly and honestly. It is what it is, so we need to accept it and then get on with life. If we handled it poorly, we need to accept our actions and try to do better in the future.

The sooner some of the more difficult lessons are learned, the more pleasant our lives will become. When life seems as black as it can be, then it can only get brighter. When things are difficult, it is because we are not aligned with the flow of the universe. We selfishly chase material rewards and accolades, which in turn cause us difficult circumstances. Once we become more attuned to the goals of the spiritual realm, our lessons will become easier and life will become more pleasant. We are like children that continue to act poorly and are always being reprimanded. We need to understand who we are and what we need to do, and life will become easier.

Enjoy Life

It is important to realize that everything will work out in the long run. We all have a tendency to fret over every little problem. Will we get to the meeting on time? What should I make for dinner? How do I look? Will people like my clothes? Does my hair look good? Then of course there are the bigger things. Can I pay the rent? Will the boss like my performance? Will my kid be OK? Unfortunately, being human means that we are prewired to worry. It is a self defense mechanism that allows us to deal with daily life, but it can also be debilitating if we let it control us.

Living a spiritual life is following our life plans. It is doing what is right, being courageous, helping others, and taking responsibility for our own actions, and it all requires putting forth effort. The lessons that we are learning, no matter how difficult they seem, are not punishments for the past, but opportunities for the future. The Universal Consciousness wants us to enjoy our journey. When life gets difficult, we need to step back and put things in perspective. We must do the best we can, deal openly and virtuously with all our issues, and then stop and smell the roses.

We will have the opportunity to experience all the lessons laid out in our life plans, and if we do not properly learn those lessons now, then we will learn them in another life. Every spirit, no matter how advanced it may be, was once at our level, and we were all once much lower. We are all progressing!

To attain inner peace and live spiritual lives, we must enhance our souls' attributes and characteristics and conquer our afflictions. We can never be fully engaged in an endeavor that brings no fulfillment of our own nature; a meaningless and purposeless way of life is rebelled against. In death we will not judge our lives on our material accomplishments, but on how we changed ourselves.

CHAPTER 9

RELIGION

Deep in the mysteries of life have I traveled,
seeking and searching for that which is hidden.

Found I that man is but living in darkness,
light of the great fire is hidden within.

– The Emerald Tablets

Key Concept:	*The clergy's focus on material possessions and power has led organized religion away from its original message.*

INTRODUCTION

Religion has been a great aid to millions of people around the globe for thousands of years. It allows us to look beyond ourselves and see a greater purpose in life. We are all continuously drawn back to the Universal Consciousness from which we came, and in our misunderstanding of truth, we mistakenly confuse that need with our religion. Unfortunately, most of the popular religions of today have strayed off message and created their own self-serving doctrines.

I began my search for truth with theology, but as I went through the various religions one at a time, at first all I found were confusion, creed, and ritual. Eventually I returned to religion, and the more I looked and the further back into history I went, the more each religion's ideas tied together, as if there was some common starting point, some universal principle where the ideas all began as a philosophy of reality.

Most of us are familiar with the major tenants of the religions we were raised in or converted to but only have hearsay knowledge of the others. As such, I have summarized my hopefully unbiased views of religion from an outsider's standpoint. This is not intended to be a complete analysis or critique of any religion, as there have been many authors who have done that in great detail, including some mentioned in the suggested reading section. The purpose of this chapter is to briefly look at the underlying messages in some of the most popular religions and see how they relate to the worldview put forth in this book.

Religion is the methodology of worshiping a deity and is characterized by eight features that are almost always present:

1. Authority

2. Ritual

3. Creed that is almost boundless and contradicting

4. Speculation on our nature and our future

5. Tradition

6. Goodness, which is the ultimate state

7. Mystery: we cannot understand it

8. Corruption: leaders exerting power over the weak

Religion can be as simple as honoring the creating principle common to all beliefs, or more complex, up to and including highly complicated creeds, rituals, and ethics specific to each one. For example, Christianity has well over two hundred sects, and each follows complicated and diverse creeds and rituals, yet they all claim to be part of the same religion. We could say the same about Judaism, Islam, Buddhism, Hinduism, and others, although, of course, the numbers of sects varies widely.

As such, I have tried to summarize the core beliefs of the following religions as I understand them, knowing full well that even slight variations are considered critical to each sect.

EASTERN RELIGIONS:

India was under the caste system well before either the oral or recorded history of any of its religions was formed. The top class consisted of the priests, and then came the warriors, followed by what we would call the middle-class businesspeople and farmers, and then came the laborers, who were followed by the "untouchables." Each caste had its own rules and obligations for living. The priests were the only class that was allowed to talk to and interface with the deities. As such, they held a special position in society. It is not known where the caste system came from, but with the priests being on the top rung of the ladder, it is not too hard to guess who the original creators were. However, in order to make the soldiers the second class, the priests must have had some pretty powerful deities on their side.

Hinduism

The first Eastern religion that we know much about is the Vedic religion. It was certainly widely followed in India before 1500 BC. The Vedas are, albeit somewhat mysteriously, considered the basis for the Hindu religion even though they contain none of the principles expounded on today. They consist primarily of four books that were put into writing somewhere over two thousand years ago. Before that time, they were passed down orally from generation to generation. No doubt much was lost over time; however, these books exist today and have been translated into most popular world languages. The interesting thing about the Vedas is that they are not and apparently never were intended to be a philosophy describing the nature of reality. Instead, they are a series of poems explaining rituals on how to worship a family of some thirty deities, which seems to have expanded over time. The poems praise the deities' deeds, actions, wisdom, and even the appearances of this family of gods. These gods have a very similar set of characteristics to other deity families like the Sumerian, Greek, Roman, and those of dozens of other cultures around the globe.

Although the Vedic texts are considered the foundation of Hinduism, there is almost no attempt to explain the origin of the world, where man came from, or where he is going. In fact, there are no ethical standards set forth outside of ritual behavior; no universal or man-made laws; no discussion of how to treat fellow humans. The only subject matter is how to behave when one is interfacing with the deities; and only the priestly class is allowed to interface with them.

These deities have very human characteristics. They are not depicted as transcendent spirits living in the heavens, although they are supposed to have originated there. They are treated as if one could visit them in their palace or elsewhere here on earth. The priests would offer them gifts and ask for favors. The gods were treated as if they were egocentric beings that loved praise and were jealous of each other, revengeful, controlling, and manipulative. They also had great powers and could protect the devotees from other deities or humans. In return for their support, these deities expected complete loyalty from their subjects; and the deities seemed to use the humans as workers on their behalf.

Sacrifices are a big part of these texts; not human sacrifices, but things that a material being would be inclined to eat or drink. Those providing the sacrifice would be instructed to leave the offerings at a specific location, usually on an altar, where the deity or representative would retrieve it. Unless the priests were consuming it all, this was a very strange request for spiritual beings that would have no need of food or drink. The Vedas are really a religion unto themselves that died several millennia ago, presumably when the deities left.

Between 1000 and 500 BC, the greatest Indian philosophers of the time decided to articulate their beliefs as to the true nature of reality, which are now captured in a set of works known as the Upanishads. The Upanishads are a collection of twelve major texts, each written separately, and each covering specific areas. This information was supposedly a secret oral teaching that may well have come down from the deities themselves. It taught that Brahman (God) was the ultimate spiritual entity, the absolute. Most importantly, it taught that each person had a self, an ego, and a body. They called the self Atman, and it was really part of Brahman. In other words, a person was an immortal spiritual entity. It explained the law of karma and stated that salvation or freedom from the Vedic cycle of life and death, called Mocksha, was achieved through wisdom of and union with the one absolute, which was Brahman, or God. Brahman lived outside the world of space, time, and causality. Brahman created the cosmos and everything in it as a divine self-concealment. The Atman was trapped in the phenomenal universe due to the ego's ignorance. It was his ignorance that caused him to view himself as separate from Brahman and to be selfish. This selfishness was the source of his fears, which in turn resulted in his suffering. Once one attained the appropriate knowledge, he could escape the cycle of karma and join Brahman in the spiritual world.

The Upanishads disagree with the Vedas in that ritual and servitude to the deities is not the path to freedom. The real enlightenment of the Upanishads was explaining that everyone, no matter what caste they were in, had an equal chance to break the karmic cycle. This was the first time that common Indians were offered the opportunity for freedom. The Upanishads are truly enlightened texts, even though some details have probably been lost over time.

The Hindu and Vedic philosophies morphed together to form a single religion, and over twenty-five hundred years ago, the Upanishads summed up Hindu philosophy as follows:

1. Vedic Hinduism was referred to as sanatana-dharma, which means the eternal nature of the soul.

2. It says that there is one supreme being[49] with no beginning or end, which can and does assume many forms.

3. The supreme being is found in the spiritual realm but also lives within all living beings.

4. It says that the individual soul is eternal, transcends the limitations of the body, and that all souls are equal.

5. Each soul has the personal freedom to make its own choices on its path of spiritual growth.

6. Maya is the illusion of the cosmos, and God created it and is within it.

---

49 Hinduism is often considered by outsiders to be polytheistic because it uses different gods to represent the characteristics of the supreme being, but that was an evolution and not always the case. Ancient Hinduism taught that there was only one God, with various aspects of the divine given specific names, but these aspects were not considered to be actual gods. They were simply key characteristics of the one and only God.

7. The soul has its own karma that follows it life after life through the process of reincarnation.

8. Each person creates his own destiny based on his thoughts, words, and deeds. In other words, we become what we think.

9. The soul incarnates through different forms until it is freed from the cycle of life and death, at which point it finally resides in the spiritual realm, regaining its natural spiritual state.

10. Vedic Hinduism allows for liberation from the life/death cycle through either the path of knowledge or the path of devotion.

This philosophy was pretty enlightened, but like so much of the ancient wisdom, over the years numerous variations have slipped into the many doctrines claiming Hindu origins.

Like most religions, Hinduism has strayed far from its original foundation. Today there is not a strict orthodoxy in Hinduism, so to say someone is a Hindu does not tell us much about that person's beliefs; however, there are a few fairly consistent principles in today's Hinduism across the various sects:

1. The three-in-one god known as Brahman, which is composed of Brahma (the creator), Vishnu (the preserver), and Shiva (the destroyer). These are commonly believed to be three separate deities as opposed to three aspects of a single deity.

2. The caste system.

3. The law of karma, which holds that good deeds invoke good effects and bad deeds invoke bad effects.

4. The law of cause and effect, which states every action or decision has good or bad consequences that will return to each person in the present or a future life.

5. The law of reincarnation, which is viewed as the transmigration of souls. This law states that each person experiences a series of physical births, deaths, and rebirths. With good karma a person can be reborn into a higher caste, and with bad karma into a lower caste, or even be born as an animal; thus the common belief in sacred bulls.

6. The goal of the Hindu is nirvana, which releases the soul from the many cycles of life and death. Nirvana is seen as either the total absorption of the ego into the divine entity with no personal existence remaining or a life with God in total adoration.

Most Hindus believe in three gods, Brahma, Vishnu, and Shiva, referred to jointly as Brahman. Some Hindus worship the wives of Shiva or one of Vishnu's ten incarnations or avatars. There are literally millions of Hindu gods and goddesses that are worshipped by the numerous sects. Hinduism also teaches that all living things are Brahman in their cores. Enlightenment is attained by becoming tuned in to the Brahman within us. Only then can one reach nirvana.

Hindus recognize three possible paths to salvation:

1. Salvation through deeds. This path's emphasis is that liberation may be obtained by fulfilling one's home and social duties and working off bad karma previously accrued.

2. Salvation through knowledge. This says our ignorance consists of the mistaken belief that we are individual selves and not one with the divine. This ignorance gives rise to our bad actions, which result in bad karma. This ignorance is overcome by deep meditation in which we realize our true identities.

3. Salvation through devotion. This requires surrendering oneself to one of the many personal gods and goddesses of

Hinduism and is expressed through acts of worship, rituals, and pilgrimages.

Hinduism was doing very well three thousand years ago, but it got off course. Unfortunately this has happened to all the major religions, although most of them were not blessed with such a good start.

Buddhism

Buddha lived around 600 BC, when the Indian caste system was already firmly in place and suffering was everywhere. Buddha considered himself a reformer of Hinduism, which at that time consisted primarily of the Vedic teachings, and he created his teaching as a protest against the corruption of the Hindu religion of his time. Buddha's main idea was to offer a relief to mankind's suffering by stating that selfishness is the cause of all suffering, and when that is extinguished, suffering ends. His principle was to offer hope to all people, no matter what their caste. It is not known whether he took this concept from the Upanishad teachings or created it himself. Although many of the Upanishad writings existed in his day, they probably were not part of the mainstream Hindu practices of the time.

Buddha said that there were four noble truths:

1. Suffering is real

2. Life does not cause suffering; only the selfish demands that we make on life do so

3. When selfishness is extinguished, peace and wakefulness remain

4. Selfishness can be extinguished by following the eightfold path:
   Right understanding
   Right purpose
   Right speech

Right conduct

Right occupation

Right effort

Right attention

Right meditation

Buddha said that since karma was a cycle, like a wheel, the eight-fold path was like spokes in that wheel. If one were to follow that path, the karmic cycle of life and death could be broken, which was Buddha's goal. The first two elements of the eightfold path consists of: (1) developing the right understanding by seeing life for what it really is, and (2) creating the right purpose for our lives, which is aligning our behavior with life as it really is. The next three are: (3) right speech; (4) right action, and (5) right occupation. The final three deal with the mind as we become what we think: (6) right effort, (7) right attention, and (8) right meditation. Defining what is meant by "right" is what Buddhism is all about, but if you use the concept that right means selfless and you concentrate on service to all, then that would probably be pretty close to Buddha's intention.

Unlike Jesus, who spent only a very few years teaching, Buddha spent forty-five years, so the body of work attributed to him is much larger and there is an amazing amount that has been written describing his philosophy. But like Jesus, his teachings were not written down until a long time after his death—150 years in Buddha's case—so some of his more esoteric ideas were surely lost or distorted.

Buddhism is like Hinduism and Christianity in that people have crafted it to suit their needs. There are two great branches of Buddhism that have emerged that are almost polar extremes: Theravada and Mahayana. Huston West[50] denotes the following differences:

---

50 Huston, *The World Religions*, page 126.

Theravada	Mahayana
Human beings are emancipated by self-effort, without supernatural aid	Human aspirations are supported by divine powers and the grace they bestow
Key virtue: wisdom	Key virtue: compassion
Attainment requires constant commitment and is primarily for monks and nuns	Religious practice is relevant to life in the world and is therefore for laypeople
Ideal: Arhat[51] who remains in nirvana after death	Ideal: Bodhisattva[52]
Buddha was a saint, a supreme teacher, and an inspirer	Buddha is a savior
Minimizes metaphysics	Elaborates metaphysics
Minimizes ritual	Emphasizes ritual
Practice centers on mediation	Includes petitionary prayer

Table 4

As these are not absolute divisions, the beliefs overlap depending on the particular teaching, so you can see how confusing this has become for the seeker of truth. Like the Vedas, Buddha believed in reincarnation of the soul and was supposed to have said: "Don't pray to me after I die, because when I am gone, I will really be gone." But that has not stopped many from praying to him anyway. Buddha believed that there was a universal thread of some sort from life to life, as the entities that we are result from previous lives and decisions made during those lives.

Buddha is also supposed to have said, "If God does not prevent evil, he is not good; and if he cannot prevent evil, he is not God." To

---

51 An enlightened being.

52 A spiritual practitioner.

Buddha, evil did not exist, nor did a personal God. However, he may have believed in a universal mind.

The ultimate goal of Buddhism is nirvana, which is a confusing and ill-defined concept. When the karmic cycle has been completed, the soul enters nirvana. Nirvana is interpreted in several ways:

1. Complete annihilation of the entity

2. Annihilation of the ego

3. Annihilation of the desire for the finite

Buddhism is unclear on what happens to the soul's identity in nirvana, as its focus is to break the karmic cycle.

To add to the confusion, Zen Buddhism has become a popular practice. Zen's aim is the attainment of enlightenment. Zen Buddhism is a methodology whereby we bypass our conscious minds in hopes of bringing our subconscious or intuitive thoughts into the conscious realm. At that time we will realize that we are part of the Universal Consciousness and therefore be able to break the cycle of life and death. It is probably true that this level of realization could be reached, but there is no way to be sure that the karmic cycle would be broken or even should be broken. We are here to learn, and when we have learned enough, the cycle ends, but not until. If the realization is our final step, fine, but if not, we continue. That said, for those that do reach this level of awareness, it can be nothing but a very positive experience, since words cannot describe ultimate truth.

WESTERN RELIGIONS OF ABRAHAM

Judaism, Christianity, and Islam all had their foundation with Abraham. He was the father figure for each religion, and he followed the deity Yahweh.

Judaism

The Torah, which consists of five chapters of what Christianity calls the Old Testament, is the history of a small clan of Semites that dates back to four or five thousand years ago. The Semites somehow got involved with a deity known as Yahweh, who traveled the world as flesh and blood, had positive and negative qualities like normal human beings, but seemed to have technologies that made him much more powerful than the Semites or their enemies. Abraham, the first of this clan to establish a relationship with Yahweh, established a pact with him.

Yahweh, who can best be described as a warrior God, seemed to have very similar characteristics to the Vedic deities, except he was much more vengeful, jealous, brutal, and angry, and required complete obedience. Yahweh purportedly killed millions of men, women, and children, which never seemed to bother him. The following passage from Leviticus[53] tells us a good bit about his views:

> *27. And if, despite this, you still do not listen to Me, still treating Me as happenstance, 28. I will treat you with a fury of happenstance, adding again seven [chastisements] for your sins: 29. You will eat the flesh of your sons, and the flesh of your daughters you will eat. 30. I will demolish your edifices and cut down your sun idols; I will make your corpses [fall] upon the corpses of your idols, and My Spirit will reject you. 31. I will lay your cities waste and make your holy places desolate, and I will not partake of your pleasant fragrances. 32. I will make the Land desolate, so that it will become desolate [also] of your enemies who live in it. 33. And I will scatter you among the nations, and*

---

53 The Complete Jewish Bible

*I will unsheathe the sword after you. Your land will be desolate, and your cities will be laid waste. **34**. Then, the land will be appeased regarding its sabbaticals. During all the days that it remains desolate while you are in the land of your enemies, the Land will rest and thus appease its sabbaticals. **35**. It will rest during all the days that it remains desolate, whatever it had not rested on your sabbaticals, when you lived upon it.* (Leviticus 26: 27-35)[54]

As atrocious as this is, it is only one of many equally outrageous statements attributed to God in the Torah and Old Testament. God is self-described in the Torah as condoning murder, rape, slavery, injustice, and about any other criminal act, sometimes for as minimal a transgression as picking up sticks on the Sabbath. The fear of his followers being attracted to other deities clearly indicates that he was but one of other powerful deities. Clearly, Yahweh had advanced weaponry that he let his followers use, which seems to have been decisive in many battles. At the same time, Yahweh tried to get his followers to live ethical, albeit often violent, lives. He was loyal to them if he perceived that they were loyal to him. But somewhere along the line he disappeared like the Vedic deities. Eventually Yahweh became synonymous

---

54 The same paragraph in the Christian Bible reads: *If after this you still refuse to listen and still remain hostile toward me, then I will give full vent to my hostility. I will punish you seven times over for your sins. You will eat the flesh of your own sons and daughters. I will destroy your pagan shrines and cut down your incense altars. I will leave your corpses piled up beside your lifeless idols, and I will despise you. I will make your cities desolate and destroy your places of worship, and I will take no pleasure in your offerings of incense. Yes, I myself will devastate your land. Your enemies who come to occupy it will be utterly shocked at the destruction they see. I will scatter you among the nations and attack you with my own weapons. Your land will become desolate, and your cities will lie in ruins. Then at last the land will make up for its missed Sabbath years as it lies desolate during your years of exile in the land of your enemies. Then the land will finally rest and enjoy its Sabbaths. As the land lies in ruins, it will take the rest you never allowed it to take every seventh year while you lived in it.* (Leviticus 26:27-35 NLT)

with the spiritual God. It seems to me that Yahweh of the Torah and Old Testament was not God, but more probably he was a deity like those described in the Vedas, only he showed very little love for humanity. Like the Eastern religions, the Western religions appear to be based on fear of the power of certain deities that were made of flesh and blood.

Judaism has evolved over time to recognize God as loving and caring, much like the Christians did, but its followers have stuck to the principle that they have a unique covenant with God that makes them special among the peoples of the earth.

The mystical aspects of Judaism described in the Zohar and other kabbalistic writings are much more aligned with the mystical doctrines of other religions but do not seem to bring anything new to the table.

Christianity

Jesus considered himself a reformer of Judaism. Christianity's chief value was changing the perceived nature of God from jealous and demanding to loving and caring. It was the implementation of Christianity by the Roman church that created the religion and at the same time sent it off course.

Christianity is based on the concept of original sin. If man was not born with sin, there would be no reason for a savior, and the fundamental doctrine would be moot. The idea of original sin is based on Adam and Eve, the snake, Satan, and the story of how Adam disobeyed God and ate the apple. For God to agree to forgive this sin of disobeying, he decided to send his son to earth to be sacrificed on the cross. This vicarious atonement is supposed to relieve mankind of the burden of sin, *provided* that each person believes that Jesus was Christ the Savior; otherwise, we are off to hell for eternity. I find this a confusing premise because according to Christian doctrine, God not only created the sinful man, but he continues to create sinful souls every time a new child is born. Somehow the sins of Adam are attached to each new child. Bertrand Russell notes that it is the soul that commits a sin, and if the soul is created fresh in every birth, how can it inherit the sins of Adam?[55] It makes one wonder why God would think that sacrificing his son, thousands of years after the incident, would atone for everyone's sins for all the years before Jesus, as those souls would not have had the opportunity to believe in this sacrifice. One also wonders why God didn't just send Jesus right after Adam ate the apple and deal with it on the spot.

For me, probably the most difficult concept in Christianity is accepting the Bible as God's word. The Bible consists of over two thousand pages of self-conflicting text. It is inconceivable to me that God would ask mankind to live by such a complicated, confusing, and inconsistent text. Additionally, the Bible has had over three hundred thousands revisions, usually motivated by attempts to refute attacks from outsiders. If God wrote the Bible through inspiration of man's hand, one would think that it would be short, concise, consistent, never in need of revision, and available to all cultures. This is strange enough, but when the first Bible was composed, few people were even literate, which put the power of God in the hands of the clergy, who created and controlled the document.

Manly P. Hall summed up his view on the Christian doctrine of salvation as follows:[56]

> "The Christian theory of redemption is unique in that it emphasizes salvation as attainable in spite of vice rather than because of virtue; in fact the divine saving virtue is accepting the divinity of Jesus Christ." " ..the church finally arrogated to itself the office of sole mediator between the spirit of righteousness on the one hand and the wayward world on the other.....consigning all

---

55 Bertrand Russell, *A History of Western Philosophy*, 458.

56 Manly P. Hall, Lectures on *Ancient Philosophy* page 145-150.

previous knowledge and beliefs of man into the limbo of decadent cults."

"It remained for Christianity to present the human race with the most indefensible and at the same time the most vicious of all superstitions, namely the doctrine of vicarious atonement—the redemption of a sinful world by the supreme sacrifice of one just man. Christ became, so to speak, the scapegoat, the sacrifice offered up that the people might go free."

"Thus a new standard of integrity was created... which could not fail to be interpreted by the unenlightened masses as evidence of the supremacy of words over works, of affirmation over action. Whereas the criers of the pagan Mysteries, according to Celsus, declared the superior worlds to be attainable only by men and women of outstanding intellect and lives consecrated to individual regeneration, the criers of the Christian Mysteries offered heaven and its eternal bliss to anyone who would confess his sins and affirm the divinity of Jesus Christ."

"How can anyone who has sensed the dignity of the Universal Plan reconcile the eternal justice of divine procedure with the right of excommunication in which the body religious ejects into outer darkness some offending hand or foot, enjoining such a soul forever from further participation in the goodness of God? How insignificant must be the power of that heaven and hell which mortal man manipulates so easily at will! Where in the realm of all that is noble and just is there a place for the concept that the souls of millions of babes are doomed to wander in the black vistas of the lost because they died in infancy without baptism? A faith cruel enough to espouse such doctrines inevitably inspires cruelty in its followers; for if it will damn its own with such unfeeling malignancy, how can it be expected to show mercy to the stranger without the gate? The survival of the church, therefore, is contingent upon its own realization of how it has mis-interpreted…the real mission of its founder…"

"It is written; "For God so loved the world that he gave his only begotten son, that whosoever believeth in him should not perish, but have everlasting life." (John 3:16) If the postulate of a personal deity is accepted then it is not unreasonable that a just creator should send a representative into the world to make known his will to man. It is not philosophically sound, however, that God should love the world more because that self same world had crucified his only begotten."

Clearly there is great wisdom in the Bible, but it seems to me the Bible was altered so much by people with special interests that it is unusable as a literal document. For example, Luke 12:47 claims that Jesus not only approved of slavery, but also approved of beating slaves. Leviticus 25:44 in the Old Testament tells us that God (Yahweh) approves of slavery as well. Tying the Old Testament and the New Testament together into one Bible was a desperate attempt to show the naysayers that Christ was prophesized. If the Old and New Testaments are both infallible and inspired, then there must be two Gods, one responsible for killing 2.5 million people and the other all loving. There are plenty of books that painstakingly explain how the Christian doctrine was created and evolved over time to address its critics and support the church and related government interests. Over the centuries and even today, Christianity has proved to be desperately autocratic by taking great pains to prevent its followers from reading materials that disparage its dogma. A good organization teaches us *how* to think not *what* to think.

But if we forget the creed and stick with Jesus's messages, then we can see where the founder may have been far more sympathetic to this book's thesis than the prevailing Christian doctrine. Christianity's biggest failure is not recognizing the divine soul in each of us. The idea that bad comes from man and all good comes from God is a message of despair. But if we read the Bible closely, we see that with all the revisions, some of the original teaching may have slipped through. In **John 10:34,** Jesus is quoted as saying, "Is it not written in your Law, *'I have said you are gods'*? and **Psalm 82:6** which says, *"You are gods, and all of you are the sons of the Most High."* Jesus had it right, but the church got it wrong. When Jesus said, *"My Father and I are one"* in **John 10:30,** he meant that his spiritual nature, and every other human being's spiritual nature, was part of the single spiritual being that I call the Universal Consciousness, or God.

As a result of the principle of God and man being fundamentally different, Christianity can not explain the concept of the Trinity, specifically the Holy Ghost. The Father is God, the Son is Christ, but who is the Holy Ghost? The Holy Ghost was certainly not man's soul, because Christianity claims: (1) the soul is born anew at every birth, and (2) the soul is born sinful so it can not be part of the divine spirit. In reality the concept of the Trinity was lifted from ancient metaphysics in which the Mother-Father was the endless eternal void or primordial soup. The Son was God that came into being out of that void. The Holy Ghost was the spirit of God that is in every living being, which is referred to in this text as the self. By making God and man different, the Christian creed eliminated the concept of the Holy Ghost. This was logically necessary, because if man was indeed part of God, how could he have sin?

Edgar Cayce was a simple man but an incredible psychic that was a devout Catholic to the day he died. For over four decades he went into a trance almost every day and gave readings about subjects that he knew nothing about in his waking hours, such as medical procedures, people's lives, history, and the future, which turned out to be amazingly accurate. Many of his readings went against his core religious beliefs, like reincarnation, with which it took him many years to personally come to grips. Eventually he was asked to go back into history and state what Jesus' message was. He said that the whole Gospel of Jesus Christ boils down to loving God and loving our neighbor as much as we love our self. If we do this we will have eternal life. This means love all our neighbors, not just other Christians.

Christ (consciousness) is the concept of loving service to all. This is a very powerful message that requires no temple, no Holy Land, no baptism, no creed. It only requires selfless service to all God's creatures.

Islam

Like all religions, Islam is divided into numerous sects that believe many different and contradicting concepts, so it is difficult to define a single set of beliefs that characterize all the Islamic religions. Unlike Christianity, Judaism, and the Eastern religions, Islam never recognized a dividing line between secular government and religion. Islamic law and state law are identical, which makes it a theocracy. There has never been a good working theocracy because it puts too much power in too few hands. It is not the concept of a theocracy that is bad, as much as it is the inevitable implementations.

Through the Koran, Islam is the word of God, and it teaches basically what Christianity and Judaism do in that it focuses on God, creation, the human self, and Judgment Day.

Islam does not believe that God has any children, so Jesus was not God's son, but they accept him as a prophet. They do not believe in the Trinity, as they believe in only one deity, which is Allah. God has fear-inspiring power, much like the Jewish Yahweh, and Muslims are taught to fear Allah. Islam believes in an uncompromising moral universe. Good and evil matter, but they do not believe in original sin or man's fall from grace. They believe man's nature is fundamentally good, but sometimes he forgets to be good and therefore requires constant reminding. They accomplish this by defining the Islamic lifestyle, which is prescribed to a great extent. Islam stresses the individuality of the soul, each of which is unique and everlasting. Man also has freedom to make good or bad decisions. Judgment Day will hold each person accountable for his actions, and God will decide if the entity goes to heaven or hell, which are vividly explained and compared in hopes of coaching the undecided. Allah is also a loving and caring God, and peace is stressed, as it is Allah's desire.

Every major task in life is identified as to whether it is forbidden, indifferent, or obligatory. This allows the Islamic communities to be either tightly or loosely controlled, depending upon the views of the leaders.

Islam believes in four major prophets:

1. Abraham, who revealed that there was only one God
2. Moses, who provided the Ten Commandments from God
3. Jesus, who taught to do unto others as we would have them do unto us
4. Mohammed, who was the principal prophet

Mohammed taught that there are five pillars of Islam:

1. There is no God but God, and Mohammed is his prophet
2. Constant canonical prayer in which one submits his or her will to God
3. Charity for the less advantaged
4. Observance of Ramadan, which lasts a month and is based on the lunar calendar, so it rotates through the secular calendar year to year

5. Pilgrimage to Mecca once in every life

Islam also teaches social laws or principles to follow:

1. Economics should stress fairness but encourage profit
2. Women are given equal status with men in the Koran, but local custom forces veils and nonparticipation in certain events
3. Race relations stress equality
4. The use of force is discouraged except for self-defense

Islam believes that submission to God's ways is the only correct lifestyle. Those who are not thankful for God's grace and do not feel an obligation to him must be punished. Islam emphasizes surrendering ourselves to God and accepting our dependence on him, and in turn gives God a total commitment to his wishes, which the clergy define.

The problem with an Islamic theocracy is obvious. It allows unscrupulous men to usurp absolute power and pretend to speak for God. The problem with a combined church and state is it attracts leaders with more ambition than integrity. Wealth brings corruption because these leaders become consumed by their selfish natures.

Like all the religions, Islam has a mystic element, known as Sufism, which teaches:

1. Love is at the center of the universe
2. The world is God in disguise
3. God is in each of us

CONCLUSION

On the surface, religion has helped many people in their searches for divine comfort. Unfortunately, instead of eradicating our fears, the distorted religious doctrines simply redirect those fears toward God's potential wrath and ultimately reinforces them for the benefit of clergy.

The real shame brought about by adhering to a religious doctrine is that we overlook the exquisite and flawless beauty of the divine plan and our role within it. By attributing the human characteristics of revenge, spite, jealousy, and intolerance to God, we bring him down to our level and make him less than he is. God would never harm us, no matter what we did, as his only feeling toward us is love, and his only concern is what is in our best interests.

At the same time that religion brings God down, it also makes us see ourselves as less than we are by having us believe that we are sinful beings in need of punishment. In truth our only weakness is ignorance, and God would never punish anyone for what they did not know. In fact, he does not judge us at all. There is no such thing as hell or purgatory, and if there were, God would not cast us into it no matter how unwisely we acted. God is all loving and has gone to great extremes to create and operate the natural and spiritual realms to ensure that we correct our misconceptions and become all wise.

The issue is not that religions speak no truth, but that the truth is veiled in a cloak of misinformation used by the selfish for the purpose of self-aggrandizement, resulting in fear and tyranny. The religious founders inevitably offered sage advice; it was the implementers that followed who were seduced by the material illusions.

Religion appeals to us because we realize that the world we see around us could not exist without some transcendent force behind it, and we can feel the pull of the spiritual world on our souls. Unlike science, which looks only at the natural realm, religion looks outside the boundaries of the universe; but in so doing they have allowed corruption to slip in, and the messages of their founders have been misinterpreted.

Salvation of the soul is: (1) the attainment of selfless service to others, and (2) the pursuit of perfection, which breaks the karmic cycle of life and death. Each of us creates his own relationship with God. Not only don't we need an advocate or intermediate, God does not permit it anyway. Each of us can and must create our own relationship with the Almighty, and in time we all will. Being an eternal entity, he patiently awaits us.

Religion rests its case upon the urgency of personal redemption, although salvation means different things to different religions. In Buddhism and Hinduism, it means an escape from suffering caused by karma. In the Abrahamic religions, salvation means life after death, living gloriously with God, including the resurrection of the body, as opposed to an eternity in hell. Philosophy and even most esoteric creeds within each religion say that there is no need for salvation because there is nothing from which to be saved. Man's only problem is ignorance, and God has put an infallible system in place in which none of his children can ever fail to become wise.

Whereas religion stresses purification of the soul through ritual and belief, philosophy stresses perfection of the soul through wisdom, love, and effort. No man can be saved by addicting himself to a religion, but it seldom occurs to the deeply religious man that salvation needs to be earned, as it cannot be bestowed. Faith over reason is always a problem.

It is man's fear that makes him addicted to religion, and it is religion's fear that makes it so intolerant. Ritual ties religion to an unchanging point in time, while the cosmos and the souls within it are continuously evolving, and inevitably religion gets left behind.

Religions fail to realize that the real sacred temple in which God resides is man himself, and the real Holy Land of all nations is the human body.

CONCLUSION

Mysteries there are in the Cosmos
that unveiled fill the world with their light.
Only by struggle and toiling the utmost
shall the star within thee bloom out in new life

All through the ages,
the light has been hidden.
Awake, O man, and be wise.

– The Emerald Tablets

My search has given me a whole new perspective on reality. I do not know who the ancients were that lived on this earth so long ago; but their wisdom that has been handed down to us in bits and pieces, and is beginning to be confirmed by science and the medical community, is as true today as it ever was. Jesus is purported to have said: "he that seeks shall find." The spiritual world may be hidden from us but it is not kept from us. It is available when we are ready for it.

Some of the deeply religious and scientifically focused people will struggle with these concepts for awhile, as will the institutions that benefit by the deceptions. But those that are ready will begin to realize that a whole new world of wisdom awaits them. In your search, don't look for proof but don't accept leaps of faith either. The answers to life come from discrimination and thought and are always the most plausible when all aspects of the issue are considered.

Our history is a myth and our myths are history. The ancients were much wiser than our culture gives them credit for. They had a much better understanding of the cosmos, mankind, and God than we do today. Unlike us, they were not burdened with selfish religions, fledgling science, and confusion over their origins.

In mankind's efforts to create a new society from the ashes of a past civilization, our selfish behavior has led us astray. We live in a world that attributes self-limiting human characteristics to God like vanity, greed, revenge and who knows what else. Not only has that instilled fear into our existence but it has led us to believe that we are inherently bad and worthy of punishment. It is important to understand that we are part of God, which allows us to join him in his eternal quest for perfection. Sin does not exist, only ignorance, and God has set up a flawless system to make us wise; and besides, no one is ever punished for what they do not know.

We all have choices as to how we live our lives. What we fail to realize is that the life we lead is a result of our past decisions. Our life circumstances are not the result of fate or someone else's efforts or successes. We are who we are because of the decisions that we have made. There is no one else to blame or give credit to but us. In turn, who we become will depend on the decisions that we have yet to make. If we want better lives, we need to make better decisions.

If we do nothing but continue as we are, eventually after living many stressful and difficult lives we will find wisdom. Everyone will succeed eventually, as God is too good and too wise to lose any of his children; but if we want to shorten the process and make our lives easier, then the onus is on us to take responsibility for our spiritual growth during this lifetime. We are not only our own worst enemy, we are our only enemy. All too often we expect the government, or our employer, or the court system, or even the lottery to make our life better. But in reality, we are the only ones capable of improving our life, as life only gives us what we deserve. We and only we are the cause of our problems and only we can resolve them.

Our worldviews are critical to helping us change our ways. If we do not understand the world we live in and our role in it we will continue to be sidetracked by the illusion. The material world offers us the false promise of worldly joy with its many material objects and personal accolades to pursue. The pursuit of these objects is a misleading goal that we need to overcome in order to find contentment. As we have seen, the world is not as it appears to be; with truth hidden in the cosmos, the world is difficult to understand. When we misunderstand the world, we make poor decisions.

Proper worldviews not only allow us to change our thoughts and our behavior, but they also allow us to change who we are. When we live lives of fear and ignorance, we make decisions that are not in our best interest. However, when we begin to understand how the world works and how we fit into it, life becomes much easier for ourselves and those around us.

We have lived many lives and died as many deaths in an effort to learn God's wisdom. We have been climbing the ladder of consciousness for eons, and yet we have only recently begun to take full responsibility for our decisions; the process is slow because the learning is thorough and complete.

The natural realm operates under a set of laws that cannot be transgressed. The law of cause and effect teaches us that every decision that is made has an effect. The universe we see around us is the culmination of all the decisions made since the beginning of creation, and its future will be determined by decisions not yet made. The law of karma, coupled with the law of reincarnation, allows for the evolution of our spirits by letting us learn from our previous mistakes and then forgetting them as they no longer have value.

When we die, we return to the spiritual world, where we review our past lives and compare them to our life plans. No one else ever judges us, as we are the sole judges of our behavior and progress. After evaluating and digesting our strengths and weakness, the pull from the cosmos eventually begins to draw us back into it again. In conjunction with our spirit guides, we then set up new life plans, in which we decide what experiences would best teach us the lessons that would be most helpful. Thought is the most powerful force in existence, and it is our thoughts that will eventually free us from this cycle of life and death. We are what we think, and as we learn more, we become more.

All spiritual beings are equal, immortal, imperfect, and searching for wisdom. Each spirit is unique because each one has had different experiences and therefore has a unique outlook on truth; as such, we each bring a unique and valued perspective to the Universal Consciousness.

Strengthening our key attributes and following our life plans is the way for us to live spiritual lives, which in turn enhances our spiritual characteristics and opens us up to realizing wisdom. The goal of existence is perfection, and the karmic force that binds us to this cycle of life and is caused by egotism. The truth we are trying to learn is about ourselves, because when we learn about us, we also learn about God.

Our ever-evolving spirits are on an endless cosmic journey of self-discovery. We are given unlimited lives in which to learn our lessons, and our only requirement is that we continually put forth effort. When we embrace our destiny and commit ourselves to the challenge of spiritual growth, then we will begin to understand and enjoy the journey. It is not so much what we think that is important, but that we cultivate the ability to think, which will enhance the unfolding of our nature.

We need to view ourselves and everything else in nature as a single entity, all part of the Universal Consciousness. What is best for others is best for us as well.

Accepting personal responsibility for our spiritual growth is paramount, as no one can take this journey for us. Aspiration toward perfection is the desire, will enables the effort, wisdom and understanding are the goals, and a virtuous life is the only choice. Life is not always easy, but it will be worth it.

God expects only one thing from us, which is to follow him toward perfection. He does not care what path we take or how long it takes us. He nurtures and guides us along the way and assists us whenever we get off course. Although he prefers that we enjoy our fascinating journey, he allows us to moan, groan, and suffer along the way, as that is our choice and is in accordance with his law of free will.

God's gift to us was life; our gift to
God is the perfection of our souls.

Akashic Records: Many esoteric philosophies and mystic elements of the major religions claim that all actions and thoughts that ever transpired on earth are contained in these records, which exist on a higher plane than the natural realm.

Alchemy: A medieval term that originated in the secret societies of Europe and was explained publicly as the chemistry of turning common metals like lead into precious metals like gold. However, within the secret societies, it had a covert meaning, in that it described the process of the soul's evolution from the crude and ignorant state of mankind into the wise and refined state of a god.

Ancient Trinity: A metaphysical concept that is similar to the Christian Trinity of the Father, Son, and Holy Ghost, only it greatly precedes it in time and differs in definition in that the Father is really the Mother-Father that was the primordial soup or chaos that existed from the beginning of time; the Son was the first spirit or God that emerged from it; and the Holy Ghost was the virtually infinite number of spirits that came from the Son and are now the Universal Consciousness.

Arhat: A spiritual being in Buddhism.

---

57 Some of these terms have multiple meanings, so these definitions are consistent with how I am using the terms.

Atman: The self in Buddhism.

Bodhisattva: An enlightened being in Buddhism.

Brahman: God in Buddhism.

Cabala: see Kabbalah.

Cosmic Cycle: Mythology tells us that God creates a cosmos, then destroys it, and then creates another one. The period between the creations of two successive cosmos is a cosmic cycle and is measured in trillions of years.

Detachment: The attitude in which we are emotionally ambiguous to the material rewards and accolades of our tasks.

Emerald Tablets: An ancient and mysterious collection of documents, although their antiquity and authenticity are questioned by many mainstream archaeologists. Occult historians generally agree that the tablets were found in a secret chamber under the pyramid of Cheops around 1350 BC. The Emerald Tablets supposedly exist as 12 tablets each created out of a single piece of green crystal and written some thirty-six thousand years ago by Thoth, the Atlantian god of wisdom. Although their true origin is lost in antiquity, the artifact was supposedly translated into Greek by Alexandrian scholars and later put on display in Egypt. They were reportedly removed from view to protect them from religious zealots who were destroying libraries around the world at the time.

Later they were said to have been carried by priests to South America and given to the Mayan culture for safe keeping. Eventually they were returned to the Giza Plateau and many believe the tablets still lie hidden there. The text is divided into fifteen sections on ten tablets, but some scholars believe that the first seven were the only original tablets and the other eight do not really exist and bogus translations were added later. The Emerald Tablets are described as rectangular green plaques with bas-relief lettering in a strange alphabet similar to ancient Phoenician. Whatever their origin and authenticity, their prophetic message is full of hidden meanings so they need to be read repeatedly in order to grasp their true meaning.

Hermetic Philosophy or **Hermeticism:** A set of philosophical beliefs that are based upon the writings attributed to Hermes Trismegistus. The Corpus Hermeticum and the Kybalion are the two bodies of work most widely known to describe this philosophy. The Corpus Hermeticum consists of seventeen books, which are set up as dialogues between Hermes and a series of others.

Illusion of the Cosmos: The perception that the material world is reality and the spiritual world does not exist.

Illusion of Diversity: The perception that all objects in the cosmos are fundamentally different and that each of us is totally separate from one another, implying that what happens to one object or being has little if any impact on another.

Illusion of Fear: The perception that we are vulnerable to the whims of the world and that death, disease, and other tragedies that befall us are random occurrences and are not in our best interest.

Incarnation: The process in which a spirit is embodied within a material object and identifies that object as itself.

Kabalion or Kybalion: A book published in 1908 claiming to espouse the essence of the teachings of Hermes Trismegistus (thought by some to be the Egyptian and/or Atlantian god Thoth), which is known as the Hermetic Philosophy. It was published anonymously by a person or group known as the Three Initiates.

Kabbalah (also spelled **Kabala** or **Cabala**): A set of mystical Jewish esoteric teachings meant to explain the relationship between God and the mortal and finite universe (his creation).

Karma: see Law of Karma.

Knowledge: The ability to perceive some aspect of the true nature of the cosmos and/or the other spiritual realms. Wisdom and knowledge differ in that wisdom is realizing emotional truths whereas knowledge is realizing rational truths.

Law of Cause and Effect: A spiritual law stating that every action is a cause that produces an effect and that everything we see around us in the entire cosmos is the effect of a previous action or decision by some being.

Law of Karma: A spiritual law requiring every mistake we make to create a circumstance showing us why it was a mistake; this is done by allowing us to experience the negative emotions we caused others so we can realize the impact of our actions.

Law of Free Will: A spiritual law that allows us to do and think what we want and therefore be responsible for our actions.

Law of Reincarnation: A spiritual law that requires us to return to the cosmos again and again in ever more advanced physical forms, enabling us to continuously evolve and perfect our souls until we are wise enough to break the karmic cycle.

Maya: The illusion of the cosmos in Buddhism.

Metaphysics: The philosophy of reality that goes beyond the natural realm and also looks for answers in a transcendent or spiritual realm.

Mind: Synonymous with spirit, it is the essence of a spiritual being. It is the element within us that thinks.

Mocksha: Vedic cycle of life and death.

Mysticism: The search for an alternative reality or worldview based on personal experiences with or intuition of God or the Universal Consciousness.

Natural Realm: The spiritual realm that we know as the cosmos or universe.

Opinion: A thought that is not truth.

Polytheism: The worship or belief in more than one deity.

Religion: A methodology of worshiping a deity, including creeds and rituals.

Self: The portion of the spirit that is divine; an element of the Universal Consciousness.

Selfishness: Any action that we commit for our own happiness that causes another person discomfort.

Soul: The portion of the spirit that is unique to the individual and retains the memory of experiences.

Spirit: The basic entity of existence, which consists of self and a soul. It is essentially a mind.

Spiritual Attributes: The innate capabilities within a spirit: desire, will, reason, emotion, creativity, and communication.

Spiritual Laws: The laws that govern the cosmos. For example: the law of cause and effect, law of karma, law of reincarnation, and the law of free will.

Spiritual Realms: The manifestations of environments created for the purpose of grouping spirits by their maturity in order to expedite and enhance their evolutionary growth.

Svabhâvat: The Sanskrit word for the elementary material within the endless void to include space and nonspace.

Theology: The study of religions.

Thoth: The Egyptian god that was known as the knowledge giver because he was supposedly responsible for giving mankind civilization. He is also believed to have lived in Atlantis and written the Emerald Tablets.

Thought: The force behind everything in the spiritual realms, including the cosmos.

Truth: The reality created by the Universal Consciousness of things as diverse as spiritual laws, beings, realms, and objects that exist. Truth is ever expanding because new things continually come into existence.

Universal Consciousness: A mind consisting of a single system of thought made up of an infinite number of individual units of consciousness or spirits all working toward the single goal of perfect understanding while embracing the guiding emotional principle of pure love toward all beings; i.e., God.

Upanishads: A collection of essays consisting of twelve major works and several minor works written by individual Hindu priests about three thousand years ago. This is the earliest known attempt by man to define God, his nature, and how mankind fits into it. Each was independently written and discusses a specific aspect of reality. Although they are sometimes considered part of the Veda literature, they are totally separate from it in content and intent.

Vedas: Ancient Indian Sanskrit texts that consist mainly of four volumes: <u>Rigveda</u>, <u>Yajurveda</u>, <u>Samaveda</u>, and <u>Atharvaveda</u>. Although they are considered to be the basis of Hinduism, they primarily consist of literally thousands of poems focused on appeasing or asking for favors from a multitude of gods, which the authors surely believed lived among them at the time.

Wisdom: The ability to feel some universal truth concerning us. Wisdom and knowledge differ in that wisdom is realizing emotional truths, whereas knowledge is realizing rational truths.

Worldview: The unique perspective that each person has regarding the nature of reality and how he or she fits into it.

Yahweh: The name of the Jewish God in the Torah and Old Testament.

Zohar: The mystical teachings of Judaism.

BIBLIOGRAPHY

Arberry, A. J., *The Koran Interpreted,* New York, Touchstone, 1955

Armstrong, Jeffrey, *God The Astrologer*, Badger, Torchlight, 2001

Bohm, David, *Quantum Theory*, Dover Publications, New York, 1951

Bohm, David, *Wholeness and the Implicate Order*, Routledge, New York, 1980

Crystal, Ellie, TheEmerald Tablets of Thoth, *www.crystalinks.com/ emerald.html,* Crystalinks, Web. July 8, 2013

Easwaran, Eknath, The Bhagavad Gita, Tolales, Nigiri Press, 1985

Easwaran, Eknath, The Dhammapada, Tomales, Nigiri Press, 1985

Easwaran, Eknath, The Upanishads, Tomales, Nigiri Press, 1999

Fisher, Joe, *The Case for Reincarnation*, Toronto, Somerville House, 1984

Frejer, Ernst, *The Edgar Cayce Companion*, Virginia Beach, A.R.E. Press, 1995

Hall, Manly P., *Words to the Wise*, Los Angeles, Philosophical Research Society, 1963

Hall, Manly P., *Lectures on Ancient Philosophy*, New York, Penguin, 2005

Hapgood, Charles, *Maps of the Ancient Sea Kings*, Kempton, Adventures Unlimited, 1966

Hawkes, Jacquetta, *The First Great Civilizations*, New York, Alfred Knopf Inc., 1973

Holy Qur'an, The: Amana Publications, Beltsville MD, 1997

Holy Vedas, The: Clarion Books, Lahore, Swan Press, 1983

Jahn, Robert G., and Brenda J. Dunne, *Consciousness and the Source of Reality*, Princeton, ICRL Press, 2011

Kramer, Samual, *History Begins at Sumer*, Philadelphia, University of Penn Press, 1981

Lama, Dalai, *The Universe in a Single Atom*, New York, Morgan Road Books, 2005

Mahãbhãrata, The, Vol. 1-5: J. A. B van Buitenen, Chicago, Univ of Chicago Press, 1978

McMoneagle, Joseph, *Remote Viewing Secrets*, Hampton Roads, Charlottesville, VA, 2000

McTaggart, Lynne, *The Field*, New York, Harper Collins, 1987

NASB Study Bible, The: Zondervan Publishing House, Grand Rapids, MI, 1999

Newton, Michael, *Journey of Souls*, St. Paul, Llewellyn, 1994

Puranas, The Vol.1-3: Bibek Debroy and Dipavali Debroy, Dehli, BR Publishing, 1994

Pike, Albert, *Morals and Dogma of the First Three Degrees of the Ancient and Accepted Scottish Rite Freemasonry*, New York, Kensington Publisher, 2004

Radin, Dean, *The Conscious Universe*, New York, Harper Collins, 1997

Russell, Bertrand, *A History of Philosophy*, New York, Simon and Schuster, 1945

Schmicker, Michael, *Best Evidence*, San Jose, Writers Club Press, 2002

Sitchin, Zecharia, The Earth Chronicles, Sante Fe, Bear and Company:
Twelfth Planet, The, 1991
Stairway to Heaven, The, 1980
Wars of Gods and Men, The, 1985
Lost Realm, The, 1990
When Time began, 1993
Divine Encounters, 1995
Lost Book of Enki, 2002
Earth Chronicles Expeditions, The, 2004
Journeys to the Mythical Past, 2007

BIBLIOGRAPHY

Smith, Huston, *The World Religions*, San Francisco, Harper Collins, 1961

Stevenson, Ian, *Unlearned languages: New Studies in Xenoglossary*, University of Virginia, 1984,

Stevenson, Ian, *Where Reincarnation and Biology Intersect*, Westport, Praeger Publishing, 1997

Tzu, Lao, *Tao Te Ching*, St. Ives, Penguin, 1963

Weiss, Brian, *Many Lives, Many Masters*, New York, Simon and Schuster, 1988

Zohar, The: Soncino Press Ltd, London, England, 1984

SUGGESTED READING

ANCIENT TEXTS

Documents from the Old Testament Times, Winton Thomas, 1958

Egyptian Book of the Dead, E. A. Wallis Budge, 1967

Enuma Elish, L. W. King, 1902

Kybalion, The, Three Initiates, 1912

Popol Vul, Dennis Tedlock, 1985

Tibetan Book on the Dead, The, 2004

ARCHAEOLOGY

5/5/2000, Richard W. Noone, 1971

African Exodus, Stringer and McKie, 1996

Ancient Cities of the Indus Valley Civilization, Jonathan Kenoyer, 1998

Cappadocia, Ömer Demir, 1993

Cataclysm, Allan and Delair, 1997

Catal Hüyük, James Mellaart, 1967

Code of the Kings, The, Schele and Mathews, 1998

Druid, The, Peter Ellis, 1996

Emergence of Agriculture, The, Bruce Smith, 1998

Epic of Gilgamesh, The, Danny Jackson, 1997

Forbidden Archeology, The, Cremo and Thompson, 1993

Giza Power Plant, The, Christopher Dunn, 1998

Journey of Man, The, Spencer Wells, 2002

Land of Osiris, The, Stephen Mehler, 2001

Lost Civilizations of the Stone Age, The, Richard Rudgley, 1999

Mapping Human History, Steve Olson, 2002

Molecule Hunt, The, Martin Jones, 2001

Mummies of Ürümchi, The, Elizabeth Barber, 1999

Mysteries of the Past, Casson, Claiborne, Fagan, Farp, 1977

Mysterious Places, Jennifer Westwood, 1997

Myth and Symbol in Ancient Greece, Rundle Clark, 1959

Origen of Language, The, Merritt Ruhlen, 1994

Search for the Cradle of Civilization, The, Feuerstein, Kak, and Frawley, 1995

Secrets of the Great Pyramid, Peter Tompkins, 1971

Serpent in the Sky, John Anthony West, 1993

Seven Daughters of Eve, The, Bryan Sykes, 2001

Seventy Great Mysteries of the Ancient World, The, Thames and Hudson, 2001

Seventy Wonders of the Ancient World, The, Thames and Hudson, 1999

Temple of Man, The, Schwaller De Lubicz, 1998

Theory of Writing, The, Andrew Robinson, 1995

Time-Life Encyclopedia of Mysterious Places, The, Ingpen and Wilkenson, 1990

Unearthing Ancient America, Frank Joseph, 2009

ASTROLOGY

Changing Your Destiny, Orser and Zarro, 1989

Cosmic Influences on Human Behavior, Michael Gauquelin, 1994

Light on Life, Defouw and Svoboda, 1996

Philosophy of Astrology, The, Manly P. Hall, 1971

Pleiadian Agenda, The, Barbara Clow, 1995

Pluto Vol. 1, Jeff Green, 2003

Story of Astrology, The, 1933, Manly P. Hall, 1933

ATLANTIS AND LEMURIA

Atlantis and Lemuria (Edgar Cayce), Frank Joseph, 2001

Atlantis in America, Zapp and Erikson, 1998

Children of Mu, The, James Churchward, 2003

Cosmic Forces of Mu, James Churchward, 1992

Dweller on Two Planets, The, Phylos the Thebetan, 1974

In Search of Lemuria, Mark Williams, 2001

Lemuria and Atlantis, Shirley Andrews, 2005

Lost Continent of Mu, James Churchward, 2001

Sacred Symbols of Mu, The, James Churchward, 2001

BUDDHISM

Gospel of Buddha, The, Paul Carus, 1987

Path is the Goal, The, Chögyam Trungpa, 1995

Spiritual Science of Kriya Yoga, The, Goswami Kriyananda, 1976

Understanding Buddhism, Gary Gach, 2009

Zen Teaching of Huang Po, The, John Blofeld, 1958

CHINESE THOUGHT

Analects of Confucius, The, Arthur Waley, 1989

I Ching, Roberta Peters, 2001

Secret of Everlasting Life, The, Richard Bertschinger, 1994

CHRISTIANITY

A Search for the Historical Jesus, Fida Hassnain, 1994

Aliens in the Bible, John, Milor, 1999

Beginnings of Christianity, The, Andrew Welburn, 1991

Book of Common Prayer, The, New York, Oxford University, 1929

Book of Mormon, The: 1991

Cipher of Genesis, The, Carlo Suarē, 1992

Dark Side of Christian History, The, Alice Walker, 1995

Essene Odyssey, Hugh Schonfield, 1984

Forgotten Books of Eden, The, Penguin Group, 1927

From Jesus to Christianity, Michael White, 2004

Genesis, E. A. Speiser, 1964

Gnostic Gospels, The, Elaine Pagels, 1979

Gnostic Paul, The, Elaine Pagels, 1975

Gospel Fictions, Randel Helms, 1988

Gospel of Mary, The, Marvin Myer, 2004

How to Understand Your Bible, Manly P. Hall, 2004

Jesus and the Lost Goddess, Freke and Gandy, 2001

Lost Books of the Bible, The, Penguin Group, 1926

Medieval Foundations of the Western Intellectual Tradition 400-1400, Marcia Colish, 1997

Misquoting Jesus, Bart Ehrman, 2005

Mystery of the Copper Scroll of Qumran, The, Robert Feather, 1999

Nag Hammadi Library, The, James Robinson, 1978

Omens of Millennium, Harold Bloom, 1996

Origin of Satan, The, Elaine Pagels, 1995

Papal Sin, Garry Wills, 2000

Purpose Driven, The, Rick Warren, 2002

Second Messiah, The, Knight and Lomas, 1997

Shroud of Turin, The, Ian Wilson, 1979

Unauthorized Version, The, Robin Fox, 1991

Woman with the Alabaster Jar, The, Margaret Starbird, 1993

CONSCIOUSNESS

Biology of Belief, Bruce H. Lipton, 2008

Holographic Universe, The. Michael Talbot, 1991

Infinite Mind, Valerie Hunt, 1989

Life and Mind, Savely Savva, 2006

Physics of Consciousness, The, Evan Walker, 2000

Self-Aware Universe, The, Amit Goswami, 1993

Thought as a System, David Bohm, 1992

EXTRATERRESTRIAL ORIGINS

Everything that You Know is Wrong, Lloyd Pye, 1998

Gods of Eden, The, William Bramley, 1989

Gods, Genes and Consciousness, Paul Von Ward, 2004

Gold of the Gods, The, Erich Von Däniken, 1973

Humanity's Extraterrestrial Origins, Arthur Horn, 1994

Mystery of the Crystal Skulls, Morton and Thomas, 1997

Origin Map, The, Thomas Brophy, 2002

Our Solarian Legacy, Paul von Ward, 2001

Prism of Lyra, The, Royal and Priest, 1989

Sirius Connection, Murry Hope, 1996

Sirius Mysteries, The, Robert Temple, 1998

Vimana Aircraft of Ancient India and Atlantis, David Childress, 1991

HERMETIC PHILOSOPHY

Hermetica, Brian Copenhaver, 1992

Secret Science, The, John Baines, 2001

Thrice Greatest Hermes Vol. 1-3, G. R. S. Mead, 1906

Way of Hermes, The, Salaman, Oven, Wharton, Mahé, 2000

HEALING

Between Heaven and Hell, Beinfield and Korngold, 1991

Buddhism and Psychotherapy, Manly P. Hall, 1979

Chinese Hand Analysis, Shifu Nagaboshi Tomio, 1996

Crystal Enlightenment Vol. 1, Katrina Raphaell, 1985

Crystal Healing Vol. 2, Katrina Raphaell, 1987

Crystalline Transformations Vol. 3, Katrina Raphaell, 1990

Encyclopedia of Magical Herbs, Scott Cunningham, 2001

Five Elements of Self-Healing, The, Elias and Ketcham, 1998

Fundamentals of Chinese Acupuncture, Ellis, Wiseman, Boss, 1991

Healing, Manly P. Hall, 1972

Honest Herbal, The, Varro Tyler, 1982

Pranic Healing, Choa Kok Sui, 1990

Rational Phytotherapy, Schulz, Hänsel, Tyler, 2000

Secrets of Crystal Healing, Luc Bourgault, 1997

Web that Had No Weaver, The, Ted Kaptchuk, 1947

HISTORICAL REVISIONISTS

Bloodline of the Holy Grail, Laurence Gardner, 2001

Fingerprints of the Gods, Graham Hancock, 1995

From the Ashes of Angels, Andrew Collins, 1996

Genesis of the Grail Kings, Laurence Gardner, 2001

Gods of Eden, Andrew Collins, 1998

Hiram Key, The, Knight and Lomas, 1996

Holy Blood, Holy Grail, Baigent, Leigh, Lincoln, 1982

Lost Keys of Freemasonry, The, Manly P. Hall, 1923

Lost Secrets of the Sacred Ark, Laurence Gardner, 2003

Lost Treasure of the Knights Templar, The, Steven Sora, 1999

Realm of the Ring Lords, Laurence Gardner, 2000

Shattering the Myths of Darwinism, Richard Milton, 1997

Sign and the Seal, The, Graham Hancock, 1992

Stargate Conspiracy, The, Picknett and Prince, 1999

Templar Revelation, The, Picknett and Prince, 1997

Underworld, Graham Hancock, 2002

HYPNOTIC REGRESSION

Between Death and Life, Dolores Cannon 1993

Keepers of the Garden, Dolores Cannon, 1993

Life After Life, Raymond Moody, 1975

Life Between Life, Whitton and Fisher, 1986

Living Your Past Lives, Karl Schlotterbeck, 1987

Mass Dreams of the Future, Chet Snow, 1989

Other Lives, Other Selves, Roger Woolger, 1987

Past Lives, Future Lives, Bruce Goldberg, 1982

MEDIEVAL HISTORY (KNIGHTS TEMPLAR)

Codex Rosæ Crucis, Los Angeles, Philosophical Research Center, 1971

Dungeon, Fire, and Sword, John Robinson, 1991

Rosslyn, Murphy and Hopkins, 1999

The Rule of the Templars, Upton-Ward, 1989

MISCELLANEOUS

Enlightenment, MSI, 1995

Illusions, Richard Bach, 1977

Mind Mastery Meditations, Valerie Hunt, 1997

On the Track of the Sasquatch, John Green, 1980

Science Frontiers, William Corliss, 1994

Book of the Sacred Magic of Abramelin The Mage, The, Mathers, 1975

Mind of God, The, Paul Davies 1992

METAPHYSICS

Discourse on Metaphysics and Other Essays, Garber and Ariew, 1991

Living Energy Universe, The, Gary Schwartz and Linda Russek, 1999

Science and the Akashic Field, Ervin Laszlo, 2007

Science of Life After Death, The, Stephen Martin, 2009

MYSTICISM

A Continuing Vision, Emanuel Swedenborg, Robin Larsen, 1988

A New Model of the Universe, P. D. Ouspenky, 1997

Ancient Secret of the Flower of Life, The, Drunvalo Melchizedek, 1998

Angel Magic, Geoffrey James, 1997

Edgar Cayce on the Akashic Records, Kevin Todeschi, 1998

Fundamentals of Esoteric Sciences, Manly P. Hall, 1965

Ghosts Among Us, James Van Praagh, 2008

Heaven and its Wonders and Hell, Emanuel Swedenborg, 2010

Isis Unveiled Vol. 1-2, Blavatsky, 1998

Lion People, The, Murry Hope, 1988

Lost Hall of Records, The (Edgar Cayce), Auken, Little, 2000

Magic, The Principles of Higher Knowledge, Karl von Eckartshausen, 1989

Ptaah Tapes, The, Jani King, 1991

Secret Doctrine, The Vol. 1-2, H. P. Blavatsky, 1999

Theosophical Glossary, Blavatsky and Mead, 1918

MYTHOLOGY

Ancient Wisdom of the Celts, The, Murry Hope, 1999

Dictionary of World Myth, Roy Willis, 2002

Myths of Narasimha and Vamana, The, Deborah Soifer, 1991

Primal Myths, Barbara Sproul, 1991

Vimana Aircraft of Ancient India and Atlantis, David Childress, 1991

PHILOSOPHY

A Brief Guide to Beliefs, Lind Edwards, 2001

A History of Knowledge, Charles Van Doren, 1991

Art of Worldly Wisdom, The, Baltasar Gracián, 2000

Divine Harmony, Strohmeier and Westbrook, 1999

Eastern Philosophy, Jay Stevenson, 2000

Essays: First and Second Series, Ralph Waldo Emerson, 1990

Great Thinkers of the Eastern World, Ian P. McGreal, 1995

Great Thinkers of the Western Word, Ian P. McGreal, 1992

Hazard, J. G. Bennett, 1976

Paracelsus Essential Readings, Goodrick-Clark, 1999

Paracelsus Selected Writings, Jolande Jacobi, 1951

Pythagorean Sourcebook and Library, The, Kenneth Guthrie, 1987

Secret Teachings of All Ages, The, Manly P. Hall, 1975

Wisdom of the Ages, Wayne Dyer, 2002

Wisdom of the Knowing Ones, Manly P Hall, 2000

Word of Will and Representation, The, Arthur Schopenhauer, 1969

World's Wisdom, The, Philip Novak, 1996

PHYSICS

A Brief History of Time, Stephen Hawking, 1988

Black Holes and Time Warps, Kip Thorne, 1994

Divine Proportion, Priya Hemenway, 2005

Edge of Infinity, The, Fulvio Melia, 2003

Hyperspace, Michio Kaku, 1995

Shadows of Creation, The, Riordan and Schramm, 1991

Tao of Physics, The, Fritjof Capra, 1991

PSYCHOLOGY

Afterlife Experiments, The, Gary Swartz, 2002

Alchemical Active Imagination, Marie-Louise von Franz, 1997

Far Journeys, Robert Monroe, 1982

Secret Vaults of Time, The, Stephen Schwartz, 1962

REINCARNATION

Old Souls, Tom Shroder, 1999

Reincarnation Controversy, Steven Rosen, 1997

Reincarnation, The Missing Link in Christianity, Elizabeth Prophet, 1997

Soul Genome, The, Paul Von Ward, 2008

Why Jesus Taught Reincarnation, Herbert Puryear, 1992

TAO

Tao, John Bright-Fey, 2006

Texts of Taoism, The, Vol. 1-2, James Legge, 1962

VEDAS

Atharva-Veda-Samhita, Vol. 1-2, William Whitney and Charles Lanman, 1905/1962

Beyond Illusion and Doubt, Bhaktivedanta and Prabhupada, 1999

Light of the Vedas, The, Manly P. Hall, 1952

Proof of the Vedic Culture's Global Existence, Stephen Knapp, 2000

Rig Veda, The, Jaroslav Pelikan, 1992

Rig Vedas, The, Penguin, 1981

Sama Veda, The, Debroy and Debroy, 1994

Secret Teachings of the Vedas, The, Vol. 1, Stephen Knapp, 1986

Vedic Aryans and the Origins of Civilization, Rajaram and Frawley, 1995

VELIKOVSKY, IMMANUAL

Ages in Chaos, 1952

Carl Sagan and Immanuel Velikovsky, Charles Ginenthal, 1995

Earth in Upheaval, 1955

Oedipus and Akhnaton, 1960

Peoples of the Sea, 1977

Ramses II and His Time, 1978

Velikovsky Reconsidered, 1976

Worlds in Collision, 1950